CHOSEN
AND
HIGHLY
FAVORED

A Woman's Sacred Call to Holiness

DIANA L. SWOOPE

Beacon Hill Press of Kansas City
Kansas City, Missouri

Copyright 2001
by Beacon Hill Press of Kansas City

ISBN 083-411-884X

Printed in the
United States of America

Cover Design: Michael Walsh

Library of Congress Cataloging-in-Publication Data

Swoope, Diana L.
   Chosen and highly favored : a woman's sacred call to holiness / Diana L. Swoope.
      p. cm.
   ISBN 0-8341-1884-X (pbk.)
      1. Christian women—Religious life. I. Title.

BV4527 .S88 2001
248.8'43—dc21

00-067501

10   9   8   7   6   5   4   3   2   1

Contents

Part 5: Communicating

Part 6: Conferring

Foreword

Not long ago at a women's convention in St. Louis, I attended a workshop led by my friend and ministry colleague Dr. Diana Swoope. She announced that she intended to publish the material presented in the workshop in her next book, to the delight of her audience. Recalling the great enthusiasm with which the workshop participants responded to her presentation, I now applaud her perseverance in producing an array of compelling portrayals of biblical women in *Blessed and Highly Favored*.

Dr. Swoope's purpose is to motivate modern readers to see the relevance of biblical women's stories to our own lives, a task she accomplishes by offering fresh and courageous interpretations of the biblical texts.

Throughout the book we encounter two lead characters who illustrate for us what it means to be "blessed and highly favored"—Mary, the mother of Jesus, and Eve, mother of all living. We also meet Elizabeth, the adviser; Naomi, the advocate; Sarah, the adversary; Deborah, the assistant; Esther, the apprentice; and the autonomous Abigail. These stories instruct us about our own spirituality and our own friendships as we observe, and prayerfully emulate, the lives of holy women.

Reverend Cheryl J. Sanders, Th.D.
Senior Pastor, Third Street Church of God
Professor of Christian Ethics
Howard University School of Divinity

Acknowledgments

Thanks to my Lord and Savior Jesus Christ who has chosen me and shown me favor.

Thanks to my very fine editor, Jeanette Gardner Littleton, and Beacon Hill Press for this marvelous opportunity to minister to women.

Thanks to the many women who inspired this writing. You don't know your names, but you appear in every paragraph of this book.

Thanks to my friend and colleague Dr. Cheryl J. Sanders. Your encouragement and support is valued beyond measure. Thanks to my adviser friends Dr. Rita Johnson and Barbara Jones for listening with patience and excitement as I repeatedly shared the concepts of this book in our conversations. Thanks to my assistant friend, Barbara Robinson, who has worked with me on each of my publications.

I especially thank my soul friend, Deborah Gayle Stone. Your encouragement and unceasing belief in me are a true gift. Thanks for praying me through this work. You are indeed a friend that sticks closer than a "sister." I value you highly.

Finally, I give thanks for my family and for their continued patience as I take on project after project. Alecia, my chosen and highly favored daughter, this is for you.

PART 1 —Chosen

1

BLESSED AND HIGHLY FAVORED

The angel went to her and said,
"Greetings, you who are highly favored!
The Lord is with you."
—Luke 1:28

Believe it or not, Luke 1:28 is the only scripture in the Bible that actually confers the status of "favored" by God upon a female. Previously only men qualified for this position: "The LORD looked with favor on **Abel**" (Gen. 4:4, emphasis added).

"**Noah** found favor in the eyes of the LORD" (Gen. 6:8, emphasis added).

"The Lord . . . showed him [**Joseph**] kindness and granted him favor" (Gen. 39:21).

"You [**Moses**] have found favor with me [God]" (Exod. 33:12).

"**Samuel** continued to grow . . . in favor with the LORD" (1 Sam. 2:26, emphasis added).

"**Jesus** grew . . . in favor with God and men" (Luke 2:52, emphasis added).

A surface look gives the impression that women are not favored by God, even in the Bible.

No female had been said to have favor with God until the virgin girl Mary received a visit from an angel. The angel's pronouncement to Mary, recorded in Luke 1, changed the whole landscape for women. Biblical writers may have left women out, but God obviously had a different idea.

Interestingly, the angel did not simply call Mary favored, but *highly* favored. When a woman was declared to have favor with or a special place in God, she was not merely called special—she was *extra*special. She did not just have the status of privileged—she was called *very* privileged.

Notice also that the announcement did not come to us through a third party. We do not normally see God speaking directly to these men. However, the angel who said, "Greetings, you who are highly favored" (Luke 1:28), plays out the scene while we read it. He personally addresses Mary on God's behalf in front of us, so to speak. And we, my sisters, are there.

We readers are a part of the angel's conversation with Mary. We hear, along with Mary, the bestowing of her newfound position. We see God directly addressing this woman as highly favored as though He, through personal mediation, was correcting a historical injustice. We're not allowed to simply read, "and Mary found favor with God." God tells Mary directly, "You are highly favored." And again, my sisters, we are there.

The angel repeats the pronouncement of favor two verses later. Often when the biblical writers repeat themselves, it's not merely for emphasis but to expand the original idea. Could these words to Mary have greater implications? Is this pronouncement of high favor for more than just this one woman? Perhaps that's why Elizabeth, Mary's cousin, was included in this conversation with the angel. Granted, the impossible pregnancy of an older barren woman helped Mary believe in the possibility of a virgin birth. Both Mary's and Elizabeth's pregnancies were true miracles.

Yet the angel's fervor about Elizabeth seems to do more than give support to a far-fetched idea. By including her, it was as if God were announcing a new status for women everywhere. Whether, young or old, single or married, fertile or barren— whatever the condition—hear the pronouncement concerning you. You have a new position—you are highly favored. This is the conferred status that I believe God wants to place on all women. Regardless of what you've experienced, be it joyful or sorrowful, you are called to be God's Holiness woman. And that calling brings privilege—special rank, most-favored status for all women who with Mary trust what God is doing in them.

This means you, my sister. You are no second-class citizen. No longer are you forgotten at the bottom of the pile. No longer are you to see yourself as a victim or an enabler. No longer are you to submerge your intelligence beneath misunderstandings of the doctrine of submission. No longer are you to hide your gifts, your God-given personality, or your feminine sensitivity. No longer must you accept disrespect simply because you're a woman. God sees you and is speaking to you as the angel spoke to Mary. And I say, even as the angel, "Greetings, to you, my sister. *You are blessed and highly favored!*"

2
A WOMAN SET APART

I was dismayed to see the flashing red and blue lights through the rearview mirror of my car. I had just returned from my morning walk in a beautiful park. I had decided to return home via a different street, where the speed limit is 10 miles lower than on my normal route.

"May I see your operator's license?" I don't know which was worse—the sight of the flashing lights or the sight of the officer standing next to my car holding a ticket pad and asking for my license and for the insurance card I'd left at home.

"Why were you in such a hurry today, ma'am?" I gave the officer what I thought was a very convincing and charming statement to solve the dilemma. He went to his car and finally returned to tell me, "You're being cited for speeding and for failure to carry a current declaration of financial responsibility in case of accident."

The officer said more, but I have no idea what. My mind scattered in a thousand different directions and rested on this point: if this incident was recorded as a point against my license, my insurance premium would rise. I did not want to pay increased insurance fees. I snapped back to reality as I heard, "Please sign next to the X."

What unmitigated nerve of this officer not to buy my story! I had explained my position. And he still wrote me a ticket. Didn't he know who I was? Even the mayor knew me. But that didn't matter. What *really* mattered was what I needed to remember: who I was and what I had been called by God to be.

I was not just the associate pastor of a large, popular church in my city. I was not just a person who had received numerous civic and community awards. None of my relationships or achievements counted. The important matter was not who I knew but who I ultimately represented—I was to be then, and always, a true and authentic representative of God's holiness in human form.

"Be holy because I, the LORD your God, am holy" (Lev. 19:2). This doesn't sound like a request from God, but sounds more like a command. It's no part-time assignment. We are to be holy all day, all week, all year—24/7.

That's a pretty scary concept, if we really think about it. Holy 24/7? Yes! Even when driving in inexplicably congested traffic, when you feel like speeding right along after the traffic clears, be holy. Even when you're cited for doing something wrong, be holy. In the midst of the heated discussion about family matters, be holy. When you're in the dressing room of the boutique and the evidences of PMS (or probably too many bags of chips with ice cream and a Pepsi) are magnified by the dress that should fit but doesn't, be holy. In the bedroom, in the boardroom, in the kitchen, in the car, wherever or whatever—our command is to *be holy*.

The God we serve is holy in every way. That's why we're commanded to be holy in every situation, every relationship, and every way. What then is this idea of holiness?

Defining holiness is difficult. First, the Bible uses the word "holy" in many different ways. Second, we find many different denominational views and perceptions of holiness and what it looks like for God's people.

I won't join the debate, but I will say God's people still need to be concerned about what He commanded the children of Israel many years ago. What does holiness mean for the new millennial Church? Or, more specifically, for a 21st-century woman whose lifestyle is very different from the women of the Old Testament but whose life issues are very much the same?

We should remember that, first and foremost, holiness is always associated with God. Holiness exists because God exists. It was not created by humans and therefore cannot be adequately defined by humans. God confers the status of "holy" upon people. We are holy only as God makes us holy, because He is the very beginning of holiness.

God declares through the prophet Hosea, "I am God, and not man—the Holy One among you" (Hos. 11:9). *God alone is the Holy One.* No one and nothing can be holy until the God who is holy touches it.

Many Christians understand holiness as moral purity or righteousness. Holiness then is mostly concerned with doing right things in right ways at the right time for the right reason. A person's actions are emphasized. Outward manifestations often become overly important in this view. Though holiness does hold an aspect of moral purity and righteousness, and though God's people should certainly be concerned with what they do, the command in Lev. 11:44 does not say "do" holy, but *be* holy. The emphasis is on *who* a person is, not just *what* a person does.

The primary meaning of the word "holy" in the Bible is "separate" or "set apart." The Levitical writer decrees, "You are to be holy to me because I, the LORD, am holy, and I have set you apart from the nations to be my own" (Lev. 20:26). Being "set apart" includes the idea of uniqueness, the quality of being so uncommon that no other counterparts exist. In a manner of speaking, we could say that to be holy is to be a "cut above."

If, for example, we were asked to name the best basketball player ever, most of us would say Michael Jordan. As a player, he was a cut above the rest. He had no equals. Or, ladies, if we were to describe the top clothing designer for the average working-class woman, we might say that Rena Rowan, Carole Little, or Liz Claiborne, depending on taste, is a cut above other designers.

The holy God of Israel, however, can go one better than them. God is not the best of a set of basketball players or dress designers. He's a cut above everyone and everything else. He's separate from, distinct from, far, far above anyone or anything else. He is separate from all other beings. No one is like Him. We see this more clearly in Exod. 15:11—"Who among the gods is like you, O LORD? Who is like you—majestic in holiness, awesome in glory, working wonders?" Nothing is common about God at all. By the same token, nothing is common about the people and things God makes holy.

3
SHE IS SACRED

You must determine between the holy and the common,
between the unclean and the clean.
—Lev. 10:10

God makes people or things holy by sanctifying, or conse-crating, them. This simply means that God, through purposeful action, sets that person or item apart solely for His service. God's touch causes the person or thing to become special, separated from the commonplace—sacred. The Levitical writer urges, "You must distinguish between the holy and the common" (Lev. 10:10).

Sacred things are defiled when they are placed in service with the common. And so are sacred people. Nothing is common about Holiness people. They are to be a cut above the rest.

Woman was set apart in the very act of creation. When God brought the female into physical reality, she was separated from Adam for a sacred and holy purpose. God consecrated her to be the "ezer," or helper, for Adam. Her calling was sacred from the very beginning.

Adam could not find a suitable helper among the animals. God never sanctioned or consecrated the animals to be Adam's suitable partner. But He did consecrate Eve. He created her while Adam was asleep, but when Adam woke up and saw her, he said, "Now this is what I'm talking about! Bone of my bone and flesh of my flesh." Eve was beautiful from the very beginning—not on-ly physically, but spiritually as well, because she was a cut above everything that Adam had ever seen (besides God). She was awe-some. She was holy. Indeed, she was *sacred.* Absolutely nothing about her was common.

God sees us as special. Yet so many Christians—especially women—have such low concepts of themselves. Many women have been made common, taking places outside of and beneath their high calling, simply because of their gender. The imposed definitions from outside and the self-imposed descriptions women accept have often kept the Eves of this world from seeing their true beauty as sacred women of God.

Woman was called out, made sacred and holy, in the very act of creation. Thus, the command that Moses gave to "be holy," spoken to the entire assembly of men and women, reminds us women are to be what we were created to be: set apart, a cut above.

Woman, look up. You are unique. Holiness is your birthright. Believe it. Become it. Bestow it upon others, for the woman God made for Adam is indeed sacred.

4
SHE IS CHOSEN

God chooses those who will be consecrated as holy. "You are a people holy to the LORD your God. The LORD your God has chosen you out of all the peoples on the face of the earth to be his people, his treasured possession" (Deut. 7:6). Think about it—of all people available on the earth, God chose the Israelites to be the nation set apart as His people. God's ultimate intent was always to bring all people under the banner of holiness through Christ's redemptive work. But to get the idea started, God chose Israel.

Why them? We don't know for sure. Just suffice it to say that there was something in them that turned the heart of God. God could have chosen many other nations that had greater qualities, were more powerful, and were larger. But Israel had something they didn't have: God's special favor. Israel was not necessarily superior, but because God loved them, they became great and powerful.

God's choice is awesome. It's not based on the criteria many think it would be. God is God. His choice is not based on our gender, looks, status, position, wealth, poverty, education, lineage, or any other such thing. God chooses because He is God.

Holiness woman, you are blessed and highly favored because the love of God is on your side! God has chosen you simply because He loves you. Think about it. Out of all of the women around, God, the Holy One, chose you to represent the glory of heaven. Your marital status does not increase or decrease your likelihood of being God's chosen vessel. Your station in life is not the reason for selection either.

So even if you have suffered abuse, God will choose you. Even if your marriage does not look like the lovey-dovey Cliff and Clair Huxtable model, God will choose you. Single mother and all, God will choose you. Though you may feel mistreated by those who should esteem you most highly, though you loathe who you are and what you've become, just remember this: God chooses you not by others' criteria, but by love. God loves you and wants you as His consecrated, chosen vessel of holiness. He created you for this purpose.

That's a pretty awesome idea by any stretch of the imagination. You're not just a means to an end. You are chosen. You are not just what will do until a better person takes the job—you are chosen. You may not have what some other sister has—still, you are chosen. And God doesn't choose to use junk.

It's time for women everywhere to rediscover and reclaim their created uniqueness. Don't submerge this concept of uniqueness under a sea of tediousness. What's so special about changing diapers? What's so special about running a children's taxicab service? What's so wonderful about being a single, childless woman? What's so super about being a supermom, superwife, superlover, even a supersaver, when all you get is super*tired*? Where is the uniqueness when no one seems to really care about me—except for what I can give them? It is found in God's love. We must learn to fully appropriate this love into our lives.

5
SHE IS LOVED

"Love the Lord your God . . . with all your mind."
This is the first and greatest commandment.
And the second is like it:
"Love your neighbor as yourself."
—Matt. 22:37-39

Biblical interpreters historically have not been kind to women. The actual portrayal of women in the Bible is not the most favorable either. Intentionally or unintentionally, when the rank and file is ordered, women tend to be found at the bottom of the order. They're often mentioned as what appears to be an afterthought and are often grouped with children in census counts. For example, when the number of people was tallied in the miraculous distribution of the two fish and five loaves, the total given was "about five thousand men, *besides women and children*" (Matt. 14:21, emphasis added).

Some people have blamed women for so much—from defiling the entire world in the Garden of Eden to being obvious antagonists deserving death, as in the story of the woman caught in adultery (John 8:3-11). Despite the fact that the Law itself demanded death to both the man and woman caught in adultery (see Lev. 20:10), only the woman was accused before Jesus and sentenced to death by stoning, as if she could commit adultery by herself.

Even in today's society, a husband who commits adultery, for example, can easily blame his improprieties on his dissatisfaction with the woman he pledged his life to "for better or for worse." He thinks he can toss her aside for "not taking care of business" as he desires, even though "business" is a partnership. An unkempt child is not that way because he or she fails to practice proper hygiene, but perhaps because his or her mother works outside the home. Women face demands to be perfect, whether assigned or assumed. The implication is that if she doesn't hold up her end of the world, the whole world will end. And in seeking this impossible goal of perfection, many women unconsciously lose themselves in the name of pleasing others. As a result, they unnecessarily loathe themselves because of others.

We need to remember we are loved and accepted by our holy Lord—no matter what. A woman doesn't have to work for it, dress up for it, be able to perform 15 tasks at the same time for it—she's just loved! Holiness is ultimately about the uniqueness of God's love for us. His love is indeed a cut above any other. Our first order of business in learning to be holy is learning to authentically love ourselves.

It's impossible to truly worship God in holiness if we don't also love ourselves. When asked what is the greatest commandment, Jesus replied, "'Love the Lord your God with all your heart and with all your soul and with all your mind.' This is the first and greatest commandment. And the second is like it: 'Love your neighbor as yourself'" (Matt. 22:37-39).

Authentically loving ourselves is crucial to authentically loving others, even God. The void created by a lack of self-love will keep us demanding that others love us exactly as we long to be loved.

We cannot give the kind of love Jesus instructed us to give, the kind that with true commitment seeks the highest good for another, without valuing and loving ourselves first. Ultimately, we will substitute others' love for something that can be filled only by God's love. We will constantly look to the objects of our love to fulfill and replenish what we gave them. This causes so much frustration in women. They seek to gain from the outside what they can only gain from the inside. They make sacrifices to obtain love only to find a deeper void. Nothing can fill this void but God's love. His love perfects our hearts so we can rightly love others as we truly love ourselves.

Sacrifice is never honest when a woman does not have true

self-love. It is bribery. I know so many women who, through sacrifice, have sought to "bribe" God into giving them people or things or positions that they prayed would fulfill what only self-love can fulfill. But as God teaches us to truly value ourselves as His chosen vessels, we find our worship of God a spiritual investment and not an emotional exchange. We also find that we can love others out of the abundance, not out of our need.

Frankly, society (and even the Church) has taught women to look for love in all the wrong places—places outside of themselves. Women have been taught that their created purpose is to love and serve everyone around them, quite often excluding themselves. The implied idea is that if women are to be in loving relationships, they must be prepared to find those relationships by losing themselves. They must submit their power to others' needs, not necessarily out of love, but out of duty.

As a result, many women have settled for whatever came along. This brings devastating results—especially as others' decisions seldom affirm the women's self-esteem and value.

However, when a woman loves herself, other people's self-serving decisions can be taken for what they are: self-serving. This enables her to interact honestly while recognizing that the results in no way measure her value or self-worth. Love knows the value of its holder. The woman who truly loves herself cannot allow disrespect, disrepute, or disdain to diminish her in any way, not even in the name of submission. She who loves and values herself, as God loves and values her, is well on the road to fulfilling the command to be holy, for to love and value oneself is "holy" indeed.

6
CREATED IN GOD'S IMAGE

To better see our true value as women, let's return to the book of beginnings, Genesis. This scripture clearly shows that women were not afterthoughts in the creation narrative. Both male and female, from the Gen. 1 account, were made in the image of God. Therefore, since both male and female were there from the beginning, both received the same instruction to be fruitful and multiply, to subdue the earth and have dominion over it.

Unfortunately, the expanded creation narrative in Gen. 2 has brought many problems for females throughout the ages. This chapter tells us that God formed woman out of Adam's side. Many believe that men have a higher human status than women since woman was fashioned from man's side. Yet, though the female was historically manifested after the man, she was created *with* the man in God's mind. Look at it from this point of view: the architect who draws up the plan for a house submits a complete plan for all the rooms of the house. The room that is built first is no greater than the one that is built second. All of the rooms are needed to make the house!

Some say woman is inferior because of the reason for her creation in the first place. Apparently, God looked at the human who was recently created and decided it was not good for the human to be alone. So He said, "I will make a *helper* suitable for him" (Gen. 2:18, emphasis added). God created woman to be a suitable helper for the man. Some interpreters believe woman's sole purpose of existing is to serve the purposes of man. Surely, a helper is inferior to, and therefore subordinate to, the one to whom she gives the help!

The Hebrew word for "helper" is *ezer*, the same word used in many other Old Testament passages to describe the help that God brings to people. Ps. 46:1 gives a prime example: "God is our refuge and strength, an ever-present help in trouble." Nothing is subordinate or inferior about God or the help He gives us. If the same word is used to describe the woman's purpose, we can make the same argument of the position she holds as a helper. What's inferior about her?

The animals were without question inferior to humans. God directed Adam to look among the animals for a helper, but he could find none, for they were common creations. Adam needed a partner who was a "cut above" the rest of creation. No creature is man's equal but woman! God separated Eve from Adam because nothing but a separated, holy woman could meet the criteria of a suitable helper for him. She is God's help to the man, his only suitable partner.

Eve's unique status clues us in to the status of all women: we are sacred, made in God's image, chosen and holy from the beginning.

7
ENTER THE CURSE

———————— ● ————————

Some of my girlfriends jokingly say when they get to heaven, the first people they want to talk to are Adam and Eve. Actually, we often discuss the seeming insanity of these two for disobeying God. One of my friends said, "All I want to ask them is, 'What in the world was wrong with you? How could you mess up like that?'" They were surrounded by perfection, with nothing more to do than live, yet somehow they managed to mess it up.

You know the story of their fall from grace. They had everything going for them. They had a luxury home in the best, albeit the only, neighborhood in the world, the Garden of Eden. Life was grand. Tend the garden, have lots of children, and make something out of the earth's resources. A wonderful life.

God only gave one prohibition: Don't eat from the tree of knowledge of good and evil. No problem, right? Wrong!

Eve ate of the fruit. Adam followed suit. And the rest is history. Say good-bye to the ritzy neighborhood and the life of perfection in God's image. Say hello to an eternal struggle to adequately reflect that image. Adam and Eve disobeyed God's commandment.

Enter the curse.

Now, because of their disobedience, God said, "Cursed is the ground because of you; through painful toil you will eat of it all the days of your life" (Gen. 3:17). Adam's work would now become harder. For Eve, childbearing would be even more difficult and painful. "I will greatly increase your pains in childbearing" (v. 16a). God also said to Eve, "Your desire will be for your husband, and he will rule over you" (v. 16c-d).

I believe Eve's punishment dealt more with her choice to follow the serpent's deceptions instead of the authority of God's word. It seems that God was saying to her, "Since you felt the need to listen to some other voice than Mine, I'll let you have your way. I'll show you the anguish and futility of depending on any other source but Me for your direction and fulfillment."

"Desire" means "to turn to" or "to look to." In other words, God was saying that since Eve did not turn to God, since she did not depend on God's authority, in her time of testing, she would now turn to Adam, her husband, for authority. Her punishment for not being dependent on God was that she would henceforth struggle with a desire to be dependent on her husband.

Eve was thus banished to a life of conflict. As much as she would want to please God in her heart, Eve would spend vast amounts of time and emotional energy desiring to please Adam. And for generations to come, women would struggle with the desire to please the men in their life rather than God.

A further consequence of this "turning" would be that each Eve to come would begin to believe that she is incapable of standing on her own, that she is inadequate as a human, incompetent to be directly led by God or to be a leader for God. She would now think she had to have a man to be somebody. Now that's a curse indeed.

Don't get me wrong. I am not saying that Eves do not need Adams. We were made for community. And before some of you close the book, this is not asking for rebellion in homes that function under the leadership of the Spirit. We must have order in community.

My sister, we were created in God's image! We were created to worship and serve God individually. Therefore, our ultimate dependence for leadership of our life must be on God. Our sole search for fulfillment and purpose must be in God.

To take the curse further, notice that *Eve's punishment was also a curse on Adam.* Eve would not only second-guess herself and turn to Adam for authority and fulfillment, but Adam would seek to rule over her in the place of God. He would now take on godlike positions in her life, not realizing what a burden it is to try to be God for someone else. Take my word for it—it's not a privilege to try to be God. It's a pain for male or female. No one is suited to be God but God alone.

The consequence of Eve's action, that she would now turn to (desire) her husband for authority and that he would respond by exercising it (ruling over her) was bad news for Eve and for all of the Eves to come.

8
THE CURSE
IS REVERSED

Poor Eve! I feel sorry for her as a historic character. She has such a bad name in religious history. She's the first woman of history and the mother of all those who came after her.

"Eve" was a very complimentary and prophetic name, meaning "the mother of all living." That's a pretty high honor for someone who just fed Adam the most costly meal he had ever eaten. He could have given her a name that reflected his disdain toward her for getting him in trouble. After all, when God asked him about the situation, he accusingly said, "The woman you put here with me—she gave me some fruit from the tree, and I ate it" (Gen. 3:12). Adam immediately blamed Eve—and God, I might add—for his dilemma. He hid behind Eve.

By the way, Eve never blamed God or Adam. She left him and God with their dignity. Sounds pretty familiar, doesn't it? It seems that women have from antiquity been willing to protect their men, even when left unprotected. When God asked her to explain her actions, Eve simply said, "The serpent deceived me, and I ate" (v. 13).

But even though Adam was willing to save his face by using his wife as a shield, he did have the good sense to name her "Eve." He didn't mark her for life by giving her a reproachful name.

Still, Eve has gotten the full blame for opening the door for sin to enter the world. She does have her responsibility. But so does Adam. In fact, God seems to have allowed some slack to Eve because she was deceived. Sin is still sin, regardless of the motives. But God is the sole judge of the intent of a person's heart. They both disobeyed God—and that is the crime for which they were punished.

Eve was punished not for usurping Adam's authority but for listening to the serpent and not to God. She followed another god when she was made to commune with the true God. That was the crime with which both she and Adam were charged and convicted. They allowed someone else to interpret God's commandment for them, when they should have interpreted it for themselves. Whenever this occurs, you are in grave danger of disobeying God.

Woman is responsible to listen to God for herself. This is her holy nature. When she ignores her call to hear God for herself by listening to someone other than God, she abdicates her holy position.

Eve was indeed responsible for committing the first action that birthed the curse of sin into the world. But God said to the serpent that Eve's offspring would birth the cure for sin as well. God said, "I will put enmity between you and the woman, and between your offspring and hers; he will crush your head, and you will strike his heel" (Gen. 3:15). This seed was Jesus.

The first Eve disobeyed God and thus received the curse of sin. But Mary, the figurative second Eve (if there's a first and second Adam, why not an analogous first and second Eve?), gave birth to the One who would bring the cure.

Jesus Christ came to the world to redeem humanity from the curse of sin ushered in by Adam and Eve's disobedience. God evidently thought women were still all right and usable. Eve's offspring would bring the remedy for sin. Mary, a virgin girl, was chosen to bring forth God's Son. This is quite a high honor, one that should not be overlooked. If women were so tainted, why didn't God choose another vessel to bring redemption? After all, God is God. If He could accomplish a birth without a man, why couldn't the same be done without a woman?

No, I believe God was saying something here. Woman was never meant to be relegated to lowly positions as a result of creation interpretations. Woman is indeed blessed and highly favored—God proved that! He gave to a woman the first promise recorded in the Bible. He promised Eve that her seed would crush the head of the serpent, that old deceiver, Satan. Sin's birth into the world brought devastating repercussions. But Christ's birth brought divine redemption.

The word "redeem" means "to buy back." The Greek word *exagorazo*, used in Gal. 3:13, has even stronger connotations than meaning "to buy out, to buy outright, with no options for repurchase." The ownership will change, and the use of the purchased commodity will too. This word was used especially to denote the buyout or purchase of a slave with the intention of giving the slave full freedom. In other words, *Christ came to reverse the effects of sin.* Sin enslaved humanity to some false concepts of our holy positions. But Christ came to set us free and return us to holiness.

For the sake of argument, let's declare that sin's curse did bring a punishment of servility and subordination for Eve. Let's say the punishment meted out in the garden did give Adam the right to rule over Eve. Let's argue further that sin wiped out all rights for all Eves ever to lead, teach, or have any authority over any Adams of this world.

But wait a minute. We must still add the redemptive work of Christ to the equation. Remember redemption? You know, that great work of Christ that released the enslaved and forever reversed their position? If Christ came to redeem us from the enslaving consequences of sin, doesn't that mean that we are restored to our original positions in God's image? Doesn't that mean that we revert to the holy and sacred status of Eve in the garden *before the Fall?* If we're still bound to the consequences of sin, then of what effect was Christ's work? Why in the world did Christ even come?

In effect, we must fully appropriate Christ's redemptive work into our lives to live according to our created purpose: holiness unto our God.

To be sure, Jesus had a much different view of women. A look at how Jesus treated women may bring greater balance and understanding.

9
THE WOMAN
JESUS KNEW

Perhaps the most authentic and telling vantage from which to view women in Scripture is through Jesus' eyes. Since Jesus often declared himself as the fulfillment of Scripture and therefore the point of reference for all scriptural interpretation, His treatment and interpretation of women is a point of reference for determining where and how women fit in the grand scheme of life.

Jesus came into a society that viewed women, more or less, as sexual objects and disposable property. They were often considered less valuable than other pieces of property owned by their husbands or fathers.

Jesus' treatment of women, however, was radical. He elevated them to the same human status as men, restoring them to their created value: sacred, blessed, and highly favored. When Jesus came along and treated women as holy vessels, the men around Him were confounded. For example, His own disciples were thrown off a bit as Jesus carried on a serious theological discussion with the Samaritan woman at the well. They were so surprised to see Him talking to a woman that they attributed His actions to delirium due to starvation, according to John 4:31.

Speaking to a woman in public was a Jewish taboo. Speaking to a *Samaritan* woman at all, in private or public, was near blasphemy. Yet Jesus not only spoke to this woman but also treated her as if she had a brain and a soul! He listened to her and responded. He talked with her enough to correct her faulty theology. She, a Samaritan woman, was invited to drink of the Living Water, to find a wellspring that would quench her spiritual thirst.

Rather than focusing on her numerous relationships, Jesus invited her into a new spiritual relationship.

Not only did Jesus speak to women in public, but He freely touched them—even women who were deemed untouchable by the Law. He was not afraid to be defiled. How can that which God has called holy defile you? So Jesus healed the woman with the issue of blood (Mark 5:24-34). He straightened the crooked back of the woman who had been bent over for 18 years (Luke 13:10-13). And in declaring this woman to be "loosed" (v. 12, KJV), Jesus gave a declaration to all women whose backs have been bent by the load of negativity heaped upon them simply because they're women.

Indeed, Jesus seemed to be quite at home with all women, because He did not view them as brainless, soulless, sexual objects. He dealt with them as human beings, equally created in God's image. His position on the value of women was perhaps no clearer than when He challenged the cultural mores on lust, adultery, and divorce. In Jesus' day, it was quite an accepted fact that men could lust after any woman with whom they came into contact outside of their own family. Actually, even in the Old Testament, when incest was a despicable offense, men lusted after and violated their own female family members, as in the case of Amnon and Tamar (2 Sam. 13).

Jesus, however, did not accept lust as a foregone conclusion that must be acted upon, but as a choice that can be controlled by the power of God's Word. He articulated His radical view on this in Matt. 5:27-28, "You have heard that it was said, 'Do not commit adultery.' But I tell you that anyone who looks at a woman lustfully has already committed adultery with her in his heart."

Adultery was not just an action perpetrated with or against women—it was an attitude held about women. Jesus challenged that attitude.

Likewise, women were also not to be regarded as expendable objects after their husbands tired of them.

It has been said, "Anyone who divorces his wife must give her a certificate of divorce." But I tell you that anyone who divorces his wife, except for marital unfaithfulness, causes her to become an adulteress, and anyone who marries the divorced woman commits adultery (*Matt.* 5:31-32).

In Jesus' eyes, marriage was a sacred institution, and so were the marriage partners. Both were to be treated with respect. Both were to honor marriage with commitment and loyalty.

Adultery was no longer to be seen as a woman's perpetration against a man. Even though the Levitical law clarified that both individuals caught in adultery were to be put to death (see Lev. 20:10), women were usually executed alone. When the teachers of the Law and the Pharisees brought the adulteress to Jesus, attempting to trap Him in their cultural tombs, His response shocked the men who brought her and the woman who fully expected to die on the spot.

If Jesus had agreed to her death, He not only would have violated the Levitical law but would have violated His own principled modeling of how to treat women. Instead of answering their trick question, Jesus doodled on the ground with His finger. I can vividly imagine Jesus writing this question: "Where is the man?" You know—the man with whom she committed adultery. How could she be caught in the act of adultery without a man involved?

I can imagine Jesus shielding what He was writing with His body so the men could not preempt His final and glorious response. Indulge my imagination for a little while longer, and picture Him completing His doodling, standing to reveal what it said while encouraging, "Any one . . . without sin, let him be the first to throw a stone at her" (John 8:7). Then, the gospel according to Swoope shows Him bending down again and writing, "Bring me the man too!" Not wanting to break the fraternal order of silence, the men left the scene one by one. More than likely, the man who committed adultery with her was one of them.

Jesus did not condone the woman's sin; all sin is a reproach, whether committed by a male or a female. Yet He affirmed that all repentant people could be forgiven, whether male or female. The woman's repentance was revealed when He said to her, "Go now and leave your life of sin" (v. 11). Though He did not actually say, "You are forgiven," we can plausibly conclude that Jesus imparted forgiveness to this previously unforgivable woman.

The Gospels forthrightly let us know that Jesus included women in His band of disciples. Luke records the names of several women who traveled with Jesus, and he alludes to the fact that many others followed Him (see Luke 8:1-3). These women were in the group of disciples when Jesus taught the great truths of the Kingdom. Including women in the band of disciples was a radical move. (Mixing men and women was Jewish taboo.) But the fact that Jesus actually took time to teach these women by answering their questions and redirecting their thoughts was nothing less than militant.

Jesus always restored women to their holy and honorable created position. They were no more holy or honored than men but were certainly no less. Jesus knew that women, submitted to Him, could have a profound impact upon the advancement of God's kingdom upon the earth. In fact, He used a woman as the first messenger of the good news of His resurrection. Women would be in the Upper Room when the Holy Spirit descended at Pentecost (Acts 1). Women would be filled with the Holy Spirit because they, from the very beginning, were made to commune with God. From the very beginning, we were to be known as God's women, blessed and highly favored.

PART 3—Communing

10

A WOMAN AFTER GOD'S OWN HEART

If asked to describe herself, the average female characterizes her life by the roles she occupies. "I'm _____'s wife." "I'm _____'s mother." "I'm _____'s sister." "I'm _____'s daughter." Women tend to describe themselves by their relationships.

Yet before we were any of these, we were women. It's easy to become so fused with our relationships that we often forget to develop a relationship with ourselves. Being holy is about being in true relationship with God and with ourselves. If our first order of business in becoming holy is to learn to love ourselves, the first step toward accomplishing this is to cultivate wholesome communion with the God who created us. Only in this place of communion do we come to truly know who we are. Communion is where we discover God's heart.

The first person with whom Eve had a relationship was God. She was under the power of His mighty, creative hand as God's vision for her unfolded into a fearfully and wonderfully made creature called woman. All of this happened apart from any other human relationship. Adam was in a deep sleep while God was developing Eve. Eve saw God's face before any other. Before she interacted with any other, she interacted with God.

Her purpose for being created was already established. Without Eve, humanity was imbalanced and incomplete. She was the other side. Since God established the purpose for Eve, only God could explain that purpose as well. Adam couldn't tell her. Some think that since Adam called her "woman," he could explain to her what it means to be a woman. Not so.

Remember this—when Adam named the animals, they already had definition. Adam could only use what he saw in them to determine a name for them. Yet when it came to finding a partner, a suitable helper, Adam didn't know what was needed. He looked at the animals and could only say, "This *isn't* it." Only God knew what "it" was. And only after God brought the woman to Adam could he say, "Whoa, man [woman]!" Adam was immediately able to see her greatness, her uniqueness. She totally awed him.

We need to directly commune with God to understand our place and position in humanity. To truly understand your identity as a holy woman of God, you must expend daily time and energy to follow after God's own heart.

11

GOD WANTS TO MEET WITH YOU

Communion with God is more than the act of prayer. True communion means walking daily under the providence of the living God, who abides in us through the Holy Spirit. Communion is showing God's power in your life. It is living in the confidence that the Spirit of God confers God's favor upon you.

Some key information about who you are can be obtained only in this type of relationship. God wants to communicate this to you directly, even as He did with Mary, the woman He chose to bear His only Son.

Mary couldn't believe that she, a lowly virgin woman, could receive a direct visit from God. Why would Mary have trouble believing that God was granting her favor? Actually, she didn't have trouble just with the concept—she had great trouble believing what the angel said about *her*.

Women have struggled with their self-worth for many, many centuries. It's amazing how many women feel isolated and lonely. I'm not talking only about single women either, but about married women as well. Why do so many of us struggle with the idea that God is indeed *with us*? Could it be that we no longer pursue communion with God, seeking to replace it with communion with man?

Interestingly, Mary had a man. She was engaged to Joseph. So if this was the end-all, be-all to high self-worth, why didn't Mary already feel blessed and highly favored? *Marriage is not the cure for loneliness—God is.* In fact, married women can be some of the loneliest people in the world! Being in the company of someone and still feeling isolated is a particularly lonely experience.

Single women don't always realize the blessing of their present state. At least you *know* you're alone.

Don't get me wrong. I'm not saying the pursuit of a godly marital relationship will always end in futility. But many married women deeply desire companionship, support, and affirmation from their mates, only to be disappointed. Why? The husband can't supply his wife's ongoing value needs. Only God can fill the chasm that exists between insignificance and value.

Long before Mary was even a thought, another woman, named Hagar, experienced a direct, unexpected visit from God. In fact, she was the first woman mentioned in the Bible, after Eve, to receive a visit from God. It appears that God has always loved and communed directly with women, even those who lived in relative obscurity. We learn of Hagar's story only because of two more famous characters, Abraham and his barren wife, Sarah. Hagar was the young Egyptian maidservant whom Sarah gave to her husband. Sarah had hoped that Hagar could give Abraham the longed-for son whom God had promised him. She had not been able to do it and thought that since she was well into her 80s, the odds were stacked against her. So Sarah decided to let Hagar have the child, and then Sarah would take him for her own.

Hagar did get pregnant, but Sarah's grand plan to be a mother backfired. Hagar's pregnancy gave her a boost of unexpected confidence, or perhaps cockiness. Pregnancy seems to do that for women. Suddenly Hagar stopped feeling like a slave girl and began feeling like a sophisticated woman. She began, the story tells us, to ridicule and scorn Sarah, taunting her with her vivacious virility, tormenting her with the thought that her pregnancy had lifted her to a place of prominence in Abraham's eyes. Perhaps she thought she was going to replace Sarah as Abraham's wife now that she was bearing his child. Another woman was possibly making the lethal error of placing her self-worth in a relationship.

That's too risky. And here's why: you're not guaranteed that even the best relationship will last until death parts you. Hagar's confidence didn't even last until the baby was delivered. Sarah put Hagar out of the house, pregnant and all, after mistreating her. Hagar fled from Sarah into the desert.

That's where God chose to visit her personally through the

angel. After instructing her to go back to Sarah and submit to her, the angel of the Lord added, "I will so increase your descendants that they will be too numerous to count" (Gen. 16:10). Then the angel said something wonderful. "You are now with child and you will have a son. You shall name him Ishmael, for the LORD has heard of your misery" (v. 11).

What makes this so amazing? Here's a single and pregnant maidservant, a person who, in all probability, would never have been known, let alone named in one of the Bible's most famous stories. Here she is, lonely in a desert place, and God not only sees her but also talks to her and gives her a promise for herself and for her offspring. In fact, she received a promise very similar to that which God had given the father of her child, Abraham: God was going to greatly increase her descendants so that they would be too numerous to count (known today as the Arab nations). God would make her son a prince, the father of many nations. The last time I checked, the mother of a prince is called a queen. She was going to move from being just a runaway slave girl to a queen—now that's a promotion!

Her son was to be named Ishmael, meaning "God hears." After the Lord said this to her, Hagar was privileged with another first. She was the first woman in the Bible to give God a name. "She gave this name to the LORD who spoke to her: 'You are the God who sees me,' for she said, 'I have now seen the One who sees me'" (v. 13). Hagar named God "El Roi," meaning "God sees."

Ishmael: God hears. El Roi: God sees. This is great news for women everywhere. Regardless of your status, God hears you and sees you. If He will appear to a runaway servant, surely He will hear you and will show you His ways.

When you know who you are, everything changes. Don't let your circumstances serve as a conclusive commentary of who you are. You're more than what you have or even what you've become. Your station in life does not determine your status with God. When you belong to God, fully and completely, you have a new name. You're no piece of junk. You're God's holy servant with a queen's inheritance. Your situation does not determine your location. El Roi sees your situation and knows how to help you find the right location within His perfect will.

12

WHOSE REPORT WILL YOU BELIEVE?

Hagar responded to God's messages about who she really was by opening her eyes from despair. She was prepared to die in the desert of Beersheba. The futility of life had gotten to her (see Gen. 21:14-16). What was the use anyway? Her child's father had put her and his son out of the house with just a morsel of bread and a vial of water. Those were now long gone. Ishmael was now 17 but had no way of supporting his mother. Who could feed her in this desolate place? Better yet, who could even see her to know that she needed to be fed? El Roi, the God who sees all!

Mary was greatly troubled when the angel pronounced her to be blessed and highly favored. Even though God's personal emissary was giving her the assurance the Lord was with her, Mary hesitated to believe the Lord's report about her. Still, the angel told her the same thing Hagar heard hundreds of years before: "Do not be afraid" (Luke 1:30). The angel then told her the wonderful news that she had been chosen to bear the son of the most high God.

The trouble with the angel's message was threefold for Mary. First, how in world did God find her in the obscurity of Nazareth and choose her for such an honor? Why not choose someone more prominent? Second, how could someone who had never been intimate with a man have a child? Miracles do happen, but this is certain impossibility. Third, who would tell Joseph, her fiancé, that his girlfriend, whom he had never touched, was pregnant? What would she say? "Oh, Joseph sweetie—I'm pregnant. It's by the Holy Spirit." Right!

Yet with all of the doubts and fears, Mary was calmed by what the angel had already told her: God is with you. God is communing with you. In fact, El Roi, the same God who saw Hagar in the lonely desert of Beersheba, also saw you and just loved you, Mary. You have found favor with God! And how would He demonstrate that favor? "The Holy Spirit will come upon you, and the power of the Most High will overshadow you" (v. 35).

God would not just talk to Mary from the outside—He would move in, by the power of the Spirit, and commune with her. Mary's outlook changed then. She saw herself for who she was. "'I am the Lord's servant,' Mary answered. 'May it be to me as you have said'" (v. 38).

What messages are you missing about yourself, perhaps because you lack daily fellowship with El Roi? Don't pretend everything is all right. The God who sees *always* sees. He misses nothing. Don't be afraid. Don't be intimidated either. All God wants to do is show you the well of water in front of you. It represents the source of life in you. Then God wants to impregnate you with life in Christ through the Holy Spirit.

13
CONSECRATION

I've said it before, but this bears repeating: first and foremost, we are women made to reflect God's face through the feminine voice. That's our holy and sacred calling. We must not forget or forsake this. It's primary. It's priority number one. Lose sight of this, and you lose everything. But lose yourself in this, and you will gain everything. Lose yourself. Consecrate yourself fully to God through a dynamic relationship with Jesus Christ. Jesus himself said, "Whoever finds his life will lose it, and whoever loses his life for my sake will find it" (Matt. 10:39).

We tend to seek God through our relationships with others. In fact, women often will unknowingly find they have compromised their relationship with God because they're chasing after others' love and affirmation, hoping to find meaningful life. We hate insignificance. Most humans do. But women especially hate the feeling of not being needed and—God forbid—not being wanted. Women love to please too. That's basic to our nature. Troubles are inevitable, however, when pleasing others becomes our unconscious reason for existing.

Consecration, on the other hand, is recognizing that God and only God deserves the place of power and prominence in our lives. Consecration is the affirmation that sin with its ugly consequences has wrested the throne of God away from our lives and buried us beneath a load of shame and guilt. Sin took us off course, but Christ returns us to the road of abundant, meaningful life by reordering our priorities and restating our purpose.

We cannot trivialize sin's effects. Because of sin, we are naturally inclined to replace God's authority by turning to men for validation and authority. As I said earlier, we women are usually pleasers. In seeking to fulfill our need to be needed, we can get so involved in pleasing others that we lose sight of the One we should ultimately please: God. We can get so entrapped in the idea that our "doing" makes us righteous that we can be deceived into thinking that even God owes us something. The doing becomes a substitute for a true relationship with Jesus Christ.

However, if we're to be truly effective, we must fully submit to the Lordship of Jesus Christ, in every way. Consecration is the conscious act of bringing self under God's authority through obedience to Christ's commands. Obedience is the key to consecration.

I don't want to be presumptuous and assume everyone reading this book has already taken the first step toward finding her real self through consecration to Jesus Christ. Let me pause to invite any reader who has not received Christ as Savior to do so. Pray this simple prayer with a sincere heart:

Lord Jesus, I admit my sinfulness and my need for a Savior. I confess that You are indeed the Savior who died for my sins. I ask Your forgiveness and seek Your help to begin a new life that is totally dedicated and committed to You. Thank You for transforming me and receiving me into the family of God. In Your name I pray. Amen.

14
EXALTATION

Through consecration, we willfully place ourselves under the Lordship of Jesus Christ. In exaltation, we joyfully place the Lord Jesus Christ over us. Exaltation is the worship of the only One who deserves such a high honor. It is the recognition that only God is fit to occupy the place of authority and authentication in our lives.

When we truly exalt Jesus Christ, we acknowledge that only because of His redeeming work are we restored to the privilege of being blessed and highly favored. Worshiping Christ is the answer to that pressing temptation to make idols out of our husbands, our friends, our children, or even our good deeds. In fact, the exaltation of Christ removes the temptation to make idols out of ourselves.

How does this happen? Let's say you prepared a sumptuous meal for your friends that cost you a lot in time, energy, and money. You're a busy single woman. You have little time, low energy, and your money is sparse. Preparing and serving this dinner caused great sacrifice to you. But they're your friends, so all you want is to make them feel valued and loved as your friends. Right? Let's see.

What if no one says, "Thank you." Or what if the dinner is acknowledged—but not as you expected? What happens then? You thought your motives were pure. But you really were hoping this gesture would endear your friends to you even more. Instead, their failure to "make over" you has left you feeling cheated, slighted, and diminished. You thought all you wanted was acknowledgment, but what you really wanted was adoration.

Yet no one deserves to be adored—not in the true sense of the word—but Jesus Christ. Christ alone restores you to your blessed position as God's holy woman. No one else deserves to be worshiped but Christ. Don't hear me wrong. I'm not saying we don't need human affirmation. I'm also not saying we can't love others deeply. And, while I'm here, let me say this—others' failure to acknowledge your works of love does not make your work any less delightful, nor does it make you any less meaningful as a person.

Exalting Jesus shows us the way out of a self-serving life. I urge you: strengthen your communion with God, and therefore your understanding of yourself, through daily worship. You don't have to wait until you're in a formal worship setting. Sing to the Lord your personal song of adoration, for as you exalt Christ, you'll learn more of how blessed and highly favored you truly are.

15
CONVERSATION

———————————●———————————

Do you remember the meaning of the name of Hagar's son, Ishmael? It means "God hears." Please underscore this: *God hears!* He hears your prayers and is attentive to your needs. So talk, sister.

I'm amazed at how many women (men too) declare they're members of God's holy family yet miss the glorious help they can receive just by talking to God. And before you begin the old "time" argument, let me take a little pressure off you. I'm talking about more than the early, wee-hour-of-the-morning prayer time your mother or grandmother always had.

God promises to listen to your prayerful interpretations about everything, including what is stressing you. And He will then tell you what you really need. Typically, our "reports" to God, which we call prayer, are skewed by our hurts, disappointments, and frustrations. God wants you to talk about these things not as information for heaven's sake, but as enlightenment for *your* sake. In your prayer times, try to spend as much, if not more, time listening than talking. You'll be amazed at what God is trying to say but can't, because of the long "shopping lists" we call prayer concerns. Hush. Listen. God is trying to tell you your real name.

The apostle Paul admonishes us to "pray without ceasing" (1 Thess. 5:17, KJV). We can be in continual dialogue with God. We women need an attitude of prayer. This will guard us from an attitude of protest when life seems grossly unfair. It also keeps us open to God's guidance at every turn. Ultimately the principle is: Talk with the Lord as you would with your most valued friend. God hears you.

16
MEDITATION

Spending time just thinking about what God is saying to you is crucial to discovering your authentic self. As Mary was bombarded by new information from the angel, from Elizabeth, and even from some shepherds, she took the time to "ponder," to meditate, to think deeply about the meaning of it all.

For many of us women, the problem is not that we don't meditate, but that we meditate on the wrong things. Be assured—you will become what you think if you think on it long enough. We treasure the wrong information. As a consequence, some bad seeds get planted in our hearts. Seeds of inadequacy and insufficiency take root. Seeds of bitterness and resentment find fertile soil in faulty meditation.

Fruitful meditation offers many benefits. It helps you examine your relationship to God, gives you correct information, and helps you see the progress of your spiritual growth. Meditation can help you piece together the meaning of your life so you will move forward to fulfill your true calling. This is the ultimate goal of meditation: to give you information that will help you obey God's call upon your life.

One of the best ways you can keep track of what you're treasuring in your heart and pondering in your mind is to keep a daily meditation journal. And again, before you discount the idea with the old "I don't have time" excuse, let me give you this thought for meditation: You don't have time *not* to do it.

Journaling helps you clearly see the progression or lack thereof in your life. It helps you to determine cyclical things in your life and others'. It can also give you a sharper perspective on how obedient you are to God's Word. Obeying God is crucial to growth.

Try it for just 15 minutes each day for one month. Choose

the time and place. Take your Bible, a notebook, and a pen. Just sit for a while and listen to God. Believe me—God will speak in the recesses of your heart. Then write down whatever you hear. Write. Don't fight. Let the thoughts flow freely. Meditate on the sermon you heard this past Sunday or on a passage of scripture to which the Lord guides you. Learn to treasure the Word of God and ponder what God says to you in your heart even as Mary did. You'll be amazed at the results.

17

DECLARATION

"How will this be," Mary asked the angel,
"since I am a virgin?"
—Luke 1:34

One thing I find so interesting about Mary's conversation with God through the angel is her stark honesty and innocence. Without hesitation, she declared her disbelief in the angel's pronouncement and acknowledged her insufficiency to accomplish the job. The fact that she was a virgin did seem to be a truly mitigating circumstance that would excuse her from accepting God's invitation to participate in this grand plan of redemption.

Some have chided our sister for registering her doubts in her ability to be the highly favored person she was labeled. But, let's be real—even with today's scientific advances, pregnancies still require male participation in some form, even if only as a biological donation. By human standards, God's request of Mary was not only absurd, but totally unfair. An unmarried woman who became pregnant in Mary's day was not put on a camel and sent to Aunt Joan's house until the birth. Women in this position were sent far away, all right—six feet under the ground, permanently!

Mary was not being doubtful—she was being honest and practical. Her question of the angel was not a statement of disbelief; it was a declaration of inadequacy. She uncovered herself before God. Amazingly, that declaration, that uncovering, enabled her to discover the means by which God intends all of us to live. "The Holy Spirit will come upon you" (Luke 1:35).

You can't get any more intimate with God than to live in communion and dependency upon God's Spirit. And the only way to truly commune with God is to be honest with your thoughts and feelings about who you are.

Declare your insecurities and inadequacies to God. Uncover the overwhelming sense of failure you feel because you're not perfect. Tell God about your sense of guilt and shame, real and imagined. Quickly confess your sins and failures. You may as well be honest. God already knows about them.

Do you want to make God smile? Daily declare your utter dependence upon Him, and open yourself to the Holy Spirit's power.

18
APPLICATION

No act of faith is complete if we don't apply what we've heard. We experience intimacy of communion with God only as we're obedient to God's commands to us. Holiness is ultimately about God's love for us. He loves you. Period. End paragraph.

You should have known there was more to it, however. Though God's love for you is not tied to what you do, but to who you are, your love for God is directly tied to what you do because of who you are. Christ said it more succinctly: "If you love me, you will obey what I command. And I will ask the Father and he will give you . . . the Spirit of truth" (John 14:15-17).

Our heroine, Mary, took a little while to come to a point of acceptance and application. We've discussed her understandable reticence and hesitation. God's command to her was truly impossible from the human vantage. Yet the angel assured her that nothing is impossible with God. Something was about to happen in Mary's life that only God could do. When she pondered the power of God to bring the achievable from the unbelievable, she landed right where God wanted her—on the point of obedience.

"'I am the Lord's servant,' Mary answered. 'May it be to me as you have said'" (Luke 1:38). In other words, Mary said, "Make of me what you will." Only then could her conversation with God end. The angel didn't leave Mary until she could say, "Your will be done."

Most of us don't pray "Your will be done" but "Your will be changed." We don't want to go through the process of application because, typically, it requires some growing in our patience.

Yet God wants to do something in your life that can end only in this affirmation: *God did it!* God's desire is always to stretch you beyond the ordinary places and positions.

God is fully aware of the difficult positions you may encounter because of your obedience. He may be asking you to forgive someone who has wounded you deeply. He may be commanding you to be still in a situation when you're feeling anxious to see its conclusion by any means necessary.

The last thing most of us want to hear is that obeying God could lead us to difficulty. Isn't it supposed to lead to blessing? Ultimately, yes. But sometimes God's commandments initially lead to more questions than they answer. Yet if you'll take the step, you'll be amazed at the final results.

By the way, ignoring God's voice won't make it go away. God persistently seeks us and insists that we do as commanded, for obedience is the pathway to truly understanding personhood and purpose. We need to echo Mary's affirmation: "I am the Lord's servant." Only then can the conversation end. For only then do we understand the purpose of God's communion with us.

19
CELEBRATION

So far we have looked at several aspects of communing with God, many of them through the eyes of Mary, the mother of Jesus. Now let's look at one final aspect vital to our fellowship with the Holy One: celebration.

Many women leave this out of the schedule for seeming lack of time or because it gets crowded out by the problems, pressures, and pains of life. Yet meditating on who God is and what He's doing results in celebration. The Holy One, with whom we were created to commune, is ushered straight to the thrones of our hearts through our celebration. The psalmist informs us that God is enthroned on our praises (see Ps. 22:3).

That injunction was not lost on Mary. Her magnificent song of praise is recorded in Luke 1:46-55. It continues to stand out as a model for any of us who may run out of ideas on what to praise our great God about.

Praising God gives you a better perspective of life. First, it reminds you that you're not operating in a vacuum. You're not grasping at straws and groping in darkness. A loving, holy God is guiding your life. Perhaps not all things are well, but this God can take all things and work them out for your good.

Celebration also makes you aware that some things are occurring in your life that God did not specifically design for you. Some facets of your life may not be due to your personal choices. You indeed may be experiencing the direct effects of someone else's foolishness and stupidity. Yet because you are connected by family, vocation, community, or association, you find yourself in a world not of your own choosing.

Still, celebration of who God is lets you see the world from a different vantage. People may intend things for evil, but God always intends them for your good, no matter how insidious the actions may be. That's a fact worth celebrating.

Mary realized that what God was doing for her was not merely a personal blessing, but one that would have positive outcomes for generations to follow. Therefore, she sang and glorified the Lord of her salvation. Praise is actually a statement of faith in the God who created you. It's an affirmation that He knows what's happening and is fully capable of bringing the best from it.

So, sister of Mary, sing your song of praise. Despite where you are, your sense of injustice, your sense of disrespect for who you are—despite all of that—God is still worthy of praise and adoration. Celebrate the grace at work in your life.

20

A FRIEND OF EVE'S

Too bad Eve didn't have a girlfriend. If she had, she probably would have been so busy talking to her that she wouldn't have had time to talk to the serpent! But surely, together they could have handled the serpent. I heard someone say there's nothing, absolutely nothing, two women can't accomplish together before lunchtime if left alone to figure it out. The only exception to that decree is if one of them is upset with her husband or boyfriend.

A true girlfriend would probably have reminded Eve of what God originally said: *Stay away from the tree of knowledge of good and evil.* But if that theological reminder didn't work, a girlfriend would probably have reminded Eve that God wasn't talking about a tree filled with chocolate—it was only a fruit tree! A real friend would have exhorted Eve to save her frivolous calories for something more delectable.

If Eve had a girlfriend, maybe, just maybe, we wouldn't be in this lifelong struggle of seeking to return to our favored and holy created state of being. But alas—she didn't have that friend. And sin messed up Eve. Let that be a lesson to all of Eve's highly favored daughters.

Some might argue that Eve had someone better than a girlfriend—she had a husband. A lot of help he was to her in her time of need, for sure. Some would go one better and say she had a greater companion than a husband—she had God. All of this is true. Still, the value of a close female friend is immeasurable. The unique challenges of being a Holiness woman in an unholy and often misogynistic world demands that we closely collaborate with those who are like us.

Women need other women. Sisters need other sisters. We need each other to affirm our highly favored positions when we're challenged by the attitudes of entitlement we face as we deal with the many tentacles of need that pull on us daily. We need someone who instinctively understands our cycles of life and can help us negotiate the circles of love to which we cling so tightly.

Nonetheless, pulpit preaching in the average church is quite often insensitive to the female's unique needs. I visited a church a few years ago with three of my sisters for a special service designed to celebrate women. At least 50 of the 75 people there were women, and about 20 were children. Use your math to determine how many men were there.

Though the church was filled with women, half of whom were single heads of households, the preacher used the occasion to discuss the evils of women hanging out together. They just gossip—that's all they do, he said. They need to be at home taking care of their children, cooking and cleaning for their husbands. He even downplayed the ambition of a woman who would dare to complete a program at an accredited institute of higher learning. This type of woman will never get a husband, he said. She's too stuck on herself.

Just when I thought the tyrannous assault was complete, the preacher sprinted toward the finish line of insensitivity. He gave his opinion on what had gone wrong with the families in America: *working women*. And his solution? Women shouldn't work outside the home. I thought, "In what life? And besides, if women aren't working, from whom will you get your next paycheck?"

The traditional understanding of holiness has taught many women to lie about their lives. In the name of holiness, women have endured partnerships that demean them as individuals and diminish their sacredness. Preaching has often admonished them to "hang in there," remaining responsible, despite the irresponsibility of those with whom they're related. Women are counseled to "be strong," though everyone around them feigns weakness. They're to run and not get weary, and keep walking even if they faint. Tired? That word is not to take even the slightest breath from their lungs. Sadly, this kind of teaching has kept Eve's daughters in a perpetual cycle of guilt and shame. From whom will she receive comfort?

Females naturally provide the comforting, nurturing breasts on which a hurting head can be laid or a hungering need can be satiated. She provides the lap on which a tired little body can sit. But by the time a female reaches adulthood, she finds no breasts on which *she* can lay or from which *she* can draw emotional sustenance. She finds no laps on which *she* can sit. Nurturing, comfort, sustenance. We women provide these things, yet we desperately *need* them as well.

Perhaps Eve did not need a girlfriend before the Fall. But after the Fall, Eve definitely could have used a friend. She needed someone who could help her understand Adam's silence and his betrayal of blaming his sin on her. She needed someone to snap her back to reality when she lamented the fact that Adam failed to protect her, and even offered her as the sacrificial lamb to God. She needed a friend to tell her that if Adam couldn't protect her then, he surely can't do it now—that only One could take care of her. And Eve would give birth to Him through her daughter Mary. They would call His name Jesus.

Eve needed a friend who would walk with her through the burden of shame she carried from the agony of deceit. The serpent deceived her. She recognized this deceitful creature for what it was, albeit after the fact. Could it be that women have a more discerning eye for this deceiver called Satan? Eve dealt a deathblow to the devil when she called him out for who he was: a rotten liar and a low-down deceiver!

A friend can stop a lie by reminding you you're not alone as you move through the seasons and stages of womanhood. She can help you hear the truth. The truth will set you free to be holy. A true friend will guard your confessions and give you covering from the embarrassment that results when your imperfections are exposed. Friends are not perfect, but Scripture says a true friend "loves at all times" (Prov. 17:17).

In order to be well "covered," women of faith need several types of friends. We'll now look at six different types and the tasks of these female friendships.

21
THE ADVISER FRIEND

Perfume and incense bring joy to the heart,
and the pleasantness of one's friend springs
from [her] earnest counsel.
—Prov. 27:9

Latin *ad* = to; *visare* = alter or *visere* = view

Eve may not have had a friend, but after hearing the astonishing news that she would be the mother of Jesus, Mary rushed to her cousin Elizabeth's house. Pregnancy is definitely a time in a woman's life when she searches out other women. Only another woman can understand the contradictions associated with pregnancy. The emotions are almost paradoxical: anticipation and apprehension, euphoria and paranoia, certainty and pesky uncertainty. The emotional temperature can change within a matter of minutes just at the sight of one's enlarged nose and spreading cheeks. Tears can instantly flow like a river, tears that only another woman can understand.

Mary had a real problem. She was definitely up against the wall, single and pregnant by the Holy Spirit! Who would believe her story? And what in the world would she say to Joseph? Mary needed someone to talk to, someone who was used to wrestling with God's directions, someone who had known disappointment but yet expected deliverance, someone who could assure her that even in this strange place, she was yet God's servant, God's chosen vessel. Enter Elizabeth.

Nothing is so wonderful as to find affirmation for your station in life in the voice of a wise counselor who has "been there and done that." Pregnant after experiencing many disappointing years of dreams deferred, Elizabeth was the most likely candidate to fill this friendship role for Mary.

When Mary arrived at Elizabeth's door in Judea, she was welcomed with the same words the angel had spoken: "Blessed are you among women" (Luke 1:42). Elizabeth's greeting shocked Mary, to say the least. But it offered just the confirmation she needed to help her fully embrace the wonder God was performing in her life.

That's what a good adviser does. She brings out of you what God has already spoken to you. She helps you embrace what you've been afraid to face. She helps you see clearly so you're free to fearlessly do God's will.

Elizabeth encouraged Mary so her state moved from questioning to singing. That's what all of us need: a mentor friend whose words are so encouraging that they release a song of gratitude and hope within us, they strengthen us for the long and arduous journeys ahead.

22
THE ADVOCATE FRIEND

Latin *ad* = to; *vocare* = call

Life has such a way of throwing us curveballs. At times we feel like Ziggy, one of my favorite comic strip characters, when he laments, "Sometimes I feel like I'm on the elevator of life, going down." Quite often it seems that just as we learn the rules of our situation, the game changes and the stakes get higher. In times like these, we're prone to hear those strange voices in our heads, voices that tell us that we're not people of favor who are deeply loved and greatly blessed by God. Problems tend to fill us with self-doubt.

Ask a woman named Naomi, whose story is recorded in the Book of Ruth and illustrates the self-doubt problems can bring. Famine filled the land where she and her family lived, Bethlehem. Their wealth could not sustain them, even in a famine. So she and her husband, Elimilech, with their two sons moved to Moab. Just as she was settling in her new city, Elimilech died. And just as she was getting used to the void caused by the loss of her husband, her two sons died.

In less than 10 years, Naomi found herself in an unimaginable place, without men in her life and therefore without an identity, so she thought. In fact, she changed her name to reflect her attitude about her problems.

"Don't call me Naomi [pleasant or favorable]," she told them. "Call me Mara [bitter], because the Almighty has made my life very bitter. I went away full, but the LORD has brought me back empty. Why call me Naomi? The LORD has afflicted me; the Almighty has brought misfortune upon me" (*Ruth* 1:20-21).

In Naomi's mind, her life ended when the lives of her men ended. That, to her, was a most empty feeling, unappeasable by anyone—even Ruth, her committed companion.

A fine feeling that must have been for Ruth, Naomi's daughter-in-law. She was there with Naomi. And what was she? A piece of chopped liver? Her husband, who was Naomi's son, had died too. Orpah, the other widowed daughter-in-law, left Naomi and returned to her people in Moab. But not Ruth. She clung to her mother-in-law, though Naomi urged her to return to her people as had Orpah. Ruth knew something of the power of an advocate friend, because her name means "a woman friend." Listen to her words, most famously spoken at many weddings though quite out of context:

> Don't urge me to leave you or to turn back from you. Where you go I will go, and where you stay I will stay. Your people will be my people and your God my God. Where you die I will die, and there I will be buried. May the LORD deal with me, be it ever so severely, if anything but death separates you and me (*vv. 16-17*).

This was a woman making a statement of loyalty and commitment to another woman. It was not to her husband or even to her children. It was to her friend. Only Ruth could truly understand Naomi's pain. She was there when it happened. She knew Naomi didn't need solutions—she needed the comfort of an advocate.

But something sacred was also at work in Ruth. She must have understood how easily the twists and turns of life can snatch our holy purpose away from us, leaving us feeling empty—with no purpose, no passion, no power, no place, no voice. Nothing.

How quickly this can happen to any of us! One unexpected accident, and the family fortune is gone. One unattended moment of passion, and the jewels of virtue are gone. One unanticipated illness, and the people you were depending on to walk with you through old age are gone. One unsuspected word, and our ministry is gone, so we think. Life can take sudden twists that propel us at warp speed into a feeling of nothingness. We feel as though we're screaming at the top of our lungs, with no sound emitted. We call out to God, but no answers come. And so, forsaken and forlorn, we just stop calling.

In times like these we need an advocate [ad] to call out [vo-care] on our behalf. We need a sister who loves at all times, who can remind us of our real name: It's not bitter—it's pleasant. We need sisters who can remind us that our worst blunder is not eternal; who, when we feel we've made a total fool of ourselves, don't think we've done a permanent job.

Ruth hired herself out as a gleaner, the lowest job on the totem pole, so she and Naomi would have food. Naomi didn't care at the time, but Ruth knew she would later. And by following God's voice to advocate on her mother-in-law's behalf, Ruth was divinely led to the field of Boaz, a relative of Naomi's. This became just the turning point needed to bring Naomi back to her pleasant self. She said of Boaz, "The LORD bless him!" She said of God, "He has not stopped showing his kindness to the living and the dead" (2:20).

It took Naomi a while to return to the holy calling inherent in her name, and it may take the person you are advocating some time as well. Yet, may I encourage you to walk with your sister and call out for her until she can call out for herself? Don't let the fact that she may reject or repel your help deter you from fulfilling your sacred mission to restore her to her holy place in God. "Let us not become weary in doing good" (Gal. 6:9). Trials, even from God's hand, are not denials of God's presence. Remind your sister of this, even as Ruth did for Naomi.

23

THE ADVERSARY FRIEND

Wounds from a friend can be trusted,
but an enemy multiplies kisses.
—Prov. 27:6

Latin *ad* = to; *vertus* = turn

"Adversary friend." Now there's an oxymoron if there ever was one. How could an adversary be a friend? Doesn't the word "adversary" mean an enemy, an opponent, the opposite of a friend? Well, it depends on how you look at things.

Remember, we're talking about the tasks of friendships. An adversary friend is one who confronts you and won't let you "off the hook" because she sees more in you than you see in yourself at the time. Her actions toward you sometimes may feel like those of an enemy, but love is her real motive. Solomon wrote, "Better is open rebuke than hidden love" (Prov. 27:5). He further notes, "Wounds from a friend can be trusted" (v. 6).

Let's set the record straight on this. When I speak of the task of an adversary friend, I'm not referring to hostile, volatile people whose actions consistently demonstrate injurious or insidious intentions toward you. These people are poisonous to your spirit and can be dangerous to your health. Flee from them. Shun them.

The task of an adversary friend is to turn us from the moronic to the heroic, from denial to determination, from fear to faith, from sin to salvation. She may need to call us to task about an unholy alliance we are forming with someone else, male or female. Her motive is not jealousy. She is simply trying to keep us from ingesting poison, lest we find no ready antidote. She may have to challenge our lethargy that's making a mockery of our spiritual gifts. *We* call it caution; without hesitation, she'll call it what it is: fear. She may passionately decry the way we belittle ourselves and live on a servant's wage when she so clearly sees our highly favored position. We mistakenly claim humility; she unmistakably comprehends our royalty and knows the two are not necessarily mutually exclusive.

If you truly want to grow in the understanding of your holy and sacred calling, do not turn from your friend who must confront you. Let her words turn you to your highest potential. And if I can challenge you further, don't throw away all of the words of your "unfriendly" critics either. Do you remember the story of Sarah and Hagar? Read Gen. 16 again.

Sarah and Hagar were certainly not the best of friends. They said some cruel things to each other. Yet those words turned out to be the impetus that propelled them both toward their godly potential. Hagar, a servant girl, found out she was the mother of a prince named Ishmael only after Sarah turned her out to the wilderness. In turn, Hagar's criticism of Sarah made her look more carefully at the promise she had already received from God. Often what is meant for evil, by an unloving critic, God will turn to (*advertus*) good (Gen. 50:20).

Think about it. How do you respond to friendly confrontation? Do you run? Do you distance yourself? Do you become testy and fight? Do you suspect the motives? Or do you seek the Lord's voice even in the seemingly hostile environment? The adversary friend can turn you to the voice of God. Listen carefully. God may be indeed be speaking.

24
THE ASSISTANT FRIEND

Latin *as* or *ad* = to; *sistere* = cause to stand

Many of the tasks to which women will be called in this new millennium will have inherent difficulties. I cannot overstate that the company we keep can make all the difference in the world as we seek to fulfill our holy agenda. As I suggested earlier, some relationships can be toxic, poisonous to your pursuit of holiness, and can deal a lethal blow to your self-concept. We've had enough to undermine us in the past. Strong women will need strong partnerships in order to stay focused on the tasks ahead.

Writing this book has convinced me of my need to have strong supporters around me. I have consulted regularly with my adviser friends and advocate friends. Two of those female friends are both advisers and advocates to me. One of them has quite often fulfilled the adversarial role and asked me the tough questions—you know, those questions that make you look over the top of your glasses, with hands on hips, giving a glare that suggests, "The nerve of you for questioning my intelligence!"

But if we truly want to be effective, we need someone who will dare to question our intelligence, someone who will take the harsh glares and the seeming rejection, if it means we will be lifted to a higher level of excellence.

Another type of female friendship that has been quite helpful to me on many projects is the supporter or the assistant friend. To be effective and experience growth, we need a friend who will support us or cause us to stand, someone who will help us with our task. When God gives you an assignment, one of the best things you can do with it is find someone who's smarter than you who can help you bring the brainchild to life. Many great ideas have fallen by the wayside because people sought to nurture these ideas in isolation.

Women especially tend to make this mistake. Women often find it very difficult to believe God speaks directly to them, giving them a unique assignment.

This is why it's so important for women to learn to share their ideas and tasks with others who can not only help them clarify and embrace their call, as Elizabeth did for Mary, but also assist them as they bring their brainchild to life.

Two unlikely partners in history were Deborah and Jael. Their phenomenal story is recorded in Judg. 4 and 5. Deborah was the wise, intelligent, well-respected judge and military leader of Israel. She lived in the hills between Ramah and Bethel (4:4-5). Her unlikely partner, Jael, lived in the plains of Kedesh in a rustic tent. Their mission? Kill Sisera, the menacing, tyrannical commander of the Canaanite army, Israel's archenemy.

Deborah had the brains, Jael the brawn; Deborah the influence, Jael the inspiration. Deborah developed the strategy, but Jael brought the victory. Initially Deborah, who had received the military command from God, tried to partner with her male military leader, Barak, but he wouldn't agree (v. 8). I'm speculating that he had a little too much male ego to follow a woman's military commands.

So Deborah essentially said to Barak, "That's OK—have it your way." But she added, "The honor will not be yours, for the LORD will hand Sisera over to a woman" (v. 9).

Deborah didn't allow the male ego or submission ideas to impede her calling. God had given her the strategy. Barak was only a part of it. Deborah would be the one held liable if she did not obey God. Barak's noncompliance didn't stop her. The consequences were too great. The judge simply went to Kedesh where Jael lived and found her to be a worthy assistant.

Deborah's strategy was to lure Sisera to the river of Kishon. Jael's tent was right on the river. Sisera would probably seek refuge there. And guess what? He did. While he was sleeping, Jael drove a stake through Sisera's temple (v. 21).

Some tasks are so monumental that you need someone

whose gifts and skills can effectively hit the nail on the head (pun intended) for you. Don't be afraid to seek someone's help, if only for the task at hand. Some friends are meant to be only for a season. Employ them. Enjoy those friends. Let them come under you and help your idea stand. And then when the time is right, move on.

25

THE APPRENTICE FRIEND

Each of you should look not only to your own interests,
but also to the interests of others.
—Phil. 2:4

Latin *ap* = to; *prehendere* = be grasped

My 16-year-old daughter relayed a telephone message to me from one of the sisters in my church. She told me, "My 'mentee's' mother called for you. She wants you to call her back."

I shockingly replied, "Your what?"

She repeated, "My 'mentee'!" It was difficult to focus on her message due to my overwhelming curiosity about this "mentee."

I then exclaimed, "You're only 16 years old, and you have a 'mentee'?"

"Sure I do. We just had a great talk."

"How old is this 'mentee?'" I thought she would tell me that the young lady was around 10 years old. Not so.

Surprisingly, my daughter explained that she had been assigned by our Follow Through Committee to mentor a 15-year-old young lady who had recently accepted Jesus Christ as Savior. A 16-year-old is mentoring a 15-year-old? What's the world coming to?

Well, if you really want to know the truth, I said to my firstborn, "Now that's what I'm talking about!" How long had I talked about giving back? How long had I preached my long, drawnout, probably long-ago-tuned-out sermon that supports the idea of reaching back to help someone. You don't have to wait until you're *over* the hill to teach someone what you know about *climbing* the hill.

Evidently my daughter hadn't tuned me out completely. At least I would like to think she appropriated the fine principles of my sermonic expertise, which allowed her to readily accept the assignment of spiritual "mentor"—although, to be honest, her youth pastor may have had more of an inside line to her missionary spirit than I. Oh, well—the woes of a parent of an adolescent. But that's another book.

Suffice it to say, one of the great needs of Christian parents is to pass on to the next generation the knowledge of their uniqueness and sacred calling. Those of us who have grasped the wonderful knowledge that we are blessed and highly favored now need to *be grasped* by someone. We need to let some young woman hold on to our skirt tail, as a baby holds on to her mother's, so she can stand tall in God's calling. It takes a woman who has apprehended her blessed created state to teach another woman how to apprehend the same. This is a part of her holy calling—to teach the following generations.

Your apprentice friend may not be up close and personal. You can mentor someone through your work, your character, your reputation, or just your story. I believe this is how Queen Vashti mentored Queen Esther—from a distance.

The Book of Esther records the stories of two queens. The first story is very short but provides the foundation for the story of the other queen. Read for yourself:

> On the seventh day, when King Xerxes was in high spirits from wine, he commanded the seven eunuchs who served him . . . to bring before him Queen Vashti, wearing her royal crown, in order to display her beauty to the people and nobles, for she was lovely to look at. But . . . Queen Vashti refused to come (1:10-12).

That's the story of Queen Vashti, the beautiful wife of King Xerxes. Her husband had given a 180-day tour of his kingdom, followed by a lavish party that lasted for 7 days. His wife was not invited to these festivities. I'm guessing he had not seen her or asked for her for 187 days! But on the last day of the party, drunk as a skunk, he decided to display the crown jewel of his possessions, his beautiful wife. She was to come to him, dressed in her royal clothes, and put the finishing touches on his royal exhibition.

But she refused to come. Vashti dared to challenge the command of the king. Honestly, Scripture gives us no indication as to why Vashti disobeyed her king's command. We have no idea why she rebelled.

But I have my beliefs. Walk with me through my speculation. I believe Vashti decided she would not display herself, like a burlesque queen, in front of his friends. She saw herself as being more than a sex object. She was a woman, not a child, to be ordered around at the selfish whims of her husband, even if he was the king. She had honor. She had dignity. And her dignity was worth more than his sovereignty!

Dignity. Choice. Self-esteem. These are worth standing up for. Queen Esther found that out. She had to have known about her predecessor, Queen Vashti.

I feel Vashti's stand made a place for Esther to stand. Esther was "apprehended" by Vashti's strength and valor. How do I know? Esther needed to see the king in order to reverse a death decree that had been issued, from his courts, against her people.

There was one problem though. The king had not called for Esther in months (sound familiar?). And it was risky for anyone to approach the king without being summoned. In fact, the person who dared to do so might be committing suicide, because the punishment for such a crime was death—unless the king decided he was willing to talk to you and extended his royal scepter, indicating that your life would be spared.

After some encouragement, more like arm-twisting, to do the right thing, Esther decided like Vashti: human dignity takes precedence over man's sovereignty. She decided to see the king, resolved that it was the right thing to do, regardless of the outcome (4:16).

So here's the moral of the story. (Every good story has one, right?) Someone is watching you, both up close and from a distance. What is she learning from you? Women need mentors who will grasp them, who will let them become an apprentice friend. They need to be grasped by your story, your spiritual strength, your self-confidence; grasped by the truth that God's woman is indeed blessed and highly favored. She is holy and sacred unto the Lord.

Who are you grasping? Who is grasping you?

26

THE AUTONOMOUS FRIEND

When all is said and done, when life has ended and eternity has begun, only one human will be left to speak for you. It's not your husband. It's not your father or mother. It's not even your best friend, your advocate, your partner, the one who would stick by you through thick and through thin.

No. In the end, *you* will be the only human left to speak for yourself. Of course, there will be God in the three manifestations: Father, Son, and Holy Spirit. The angels will be there, and so will the other departed saints. But no one will be able to speak for you but you. That's deep, huh?

"What are you saying, Lady Di?" (That's what my friends call me.) I'm glad you asked. As much as we need friends who will provide us with comfort, counsel, critique, collaboration, and constructive channeling of our energies, the person you really need as the ultimate best friend is—you guessed it—you!

Let's face it. Friends, as good as they are, can disappoint. They move. They get caught up with their own agendas and needs.

Even the biblical women, whose stories we have heard in previous chapters, found friends could go only so far. Mary found a great friend and adviser in Elizabeth. Still, only Mary could bring forth the Christ child conceived in her by the Holy Spirit. Ruth spoke up for Naomi and protected her as she lived under her assumed name, Mara. However, Naomi herself had to finally release her bitterness and reclaim the joy inherent in her pleasant name.

Hagar blindly fled from Sarah's criticism into a wilderness of despair. Though driven by blind criticism, Hagar personally discovered and named El Roi, the God who was far from blind. Jael may have been the one to cause Deborah's strategy to stand. Sisera, however, found that Jael was quite capable of staking her own claim to divine direction. Esther probably learned from Vashti's story and was inspired by her strength. But Vashti could not go with her into the king's court. Esther had to go alone.

The question is: Do you feed your own soul? Do you guard your own dignity? Do you avoid taking less than what you should? Do you rest when you're sick, or do you push on in the name of Jesus?

God loved you so much when He created you that He gave you a unique personality, a unique set of gifts, a unique calling. You were to be a one-of-a-kind expression of God's image. To deny this is to deny the gift of God within you.

Our world has such a desperate need for holy people, holy women who are empowered from within; women who, because they understand their power in Christ, can unleash the power of Christ in others. Our friends can help us grow in self-understanding as it relates to Christ's call. But ultimately, each woman will have to grapple with her own set of circumstances, finding ways to personally apprehend God's power.

Sometimes application and tradition may clash as we seek to find God's will for our lives. A great story in the Old Testament supports this idea. A woman named Abigail demonstrates the principle of the autonomous friend. As you will see, she was her own best friend.

> A certain man in Maon, who had property there at Carmel, was very wealthy. He had a thousand goats and three thousand sheep, which he was shearing in Carmel.

> His name was Nabal and his wife's name was Abigail. She was an intelligent and beautiful woman, but her husband, a Calebite, was surly and mean in his dealings (*1 Sam.* 25:2-3).

Already this story is shaping up for disaster—Abigail, whose name means "joy," is married to a man named Nabal, which means "fool." An intelligent, beautiful, joyful woman somehow has been joined in marriage to a mean, selfish, "surly" fool. How did she make it?

My speculation is that she learned to separate herself from the foolishness. Somewhere in her mind she must have decided that she was "through with the dumb stuff." She was not a product of Nabal's actions, and he was not a reflection of her personality. Abigail was joined to a fool, but she did not feel the need to accept his invitations to join him in his foolishness.

Point in case: Nabal decided he would be mean to David, the mighty warrior and future king of Israel. I won't recount the whole story here—you'll need to read it in 1 Sam. 25.

Here's the short of it. David and his men had protected Nabal's sheep shearers from attack and robbery for several months. They did this without pay simply because David was so kindhearted. One day David needed some assistance from Nabal. All he wanted was a little bread and water for his men, something that would be a drop in the bucket for such a wealthy man as Nabal.

But guess what? Nabal refused David. You heard me—*he refused David.* Lion and bear-killing David. Slingshot-wielding, expert swashbuckler, Goliath-killing David. How foolish can you get? Obviously very foolish if your name is Nabal.

Unfortunately, kindness ran out when meanness ran in. David promised to kill Nabal and all his household for this grave injustice. A servant told Abigail about David's intentions. Fortunately for her, wisdom prevailed where foolishness assailed. Abigail geared up for action.

When she went to David, she didn't try to paint a bright picture or cover up for her husband. She went to plead for mercy for herself. She did it by using the truth, and the truth set her free. David accepted her mediation and called off the militia. By the way, Abigail did not tell her husband until after she had enacted her plan of mediation. Let that be a lesson to some of you, my readers. Some things are best left unsaid until they cannot be undone. Wisdom may dictate that you act independently of foolish, selfish people, for your sake and for those you represent. It does not matter what the person's place or position is in your life. Putting your God-given plan in the hands of a fool is not wise—in fact, it could even mean your death.

Remember that God has a holy agenda for your life. You cannot afford to let anyone, no matter what the relation, impede your acceptance of that calling. To do so relegates you to the Nabal level. Yet if you will follow wisdom, it's amazing how God will protect you and provide for your future.

Nabal had a heart attack and became like a stone when Abigail finally told him what happened. Ten days later, he was dead. When David found out that Nabal was out of the way, he sent some messengers to bring Abigail back to him. He wanted to marry her. Abigail heard that news and "quickly got on a donkey and . . . went with David's messengers and became his wife" (1 Sam. 25:42). She had no time for *mourning*. God had ushered her into the *morning*!

Life is filled with trepidation. Fulfilling your holy agenda will not always be easy, especially if you are surrounded by a great cloud of idiots like Nabal. Yet God calls you to make choices that will empower you. Sometimes they may go against convention. Sometimes you'll feel as though you betrayed your partners. But remember—self-betrayal is the worst kind of betrayal.

Don't miss your Abigail blessing by lamenting your partnerships. You don't necessarily need to physically divorce yourself from these people. Yet you don't have to join yourself to their foolish decisions, foolish ethics, foolish actions, or just plain downright foolishness. Let fools take the low road. You take the high road. You're a "cut above." You've already been separated and set apart. What God has separated let no one join back together. Amen!

PART 5—Communicating

27
IT'S TIME TO STEP UP!

Most people who know me know I'm a big fan of basketball. I was watching an NCAA basketball championship game a little while ago. The reigning championship team was widely heralded as the sure victor in this contest. For quite a while the underdog team played head-to-head with the champions, but they eventually fell behind. Just when it seemed as though the challengers would be routed by the champions, I saw one of their star players point to a teammate and shout, "It's time to step up! It's winning time!" Those two players "stepped up" and literally took the championship from the incumbents.

This is what we must do in these last days. *Sister, it's time to step up!* Too many of God's blessed and highly favored women are being routed by the reigning champion of the world of darkness—Satan himself. It's time for those of us who have the Holy Spirit of God at work in us to rise and take over in the name of Jesus.

If I sound radical and have by some means found a way to rattle you, then I thank God—my words are not returning void. We've spent too much time being nice while the enemy is running rampant through our homes, communities, and even our churches. The divorce rate among Holiness people is the same as that of society. Almost as many people are committing adultery, addicted to bad relationships, and living defenseless, defeated lives in the

Church as outside the Church. If Holiness people face life the same way as the world, what difference does holiness make?

We're called to be in the world but not of the world (John 17). We tend to major on the "not of the world" part of that passage (v. 16). Yet we must remember that God calls Holiness people to be *in* the world as well.

Remember God has given you the blessing of Mary—you're highly favored. But your blessing is not just for you. You have a job to do. You have been blessed so you can communicate God's power to others. Your authentic witness is needed to bring God's compassionate presence alive in the world.

While a holy character is our *defense* against hypocrisy and corruption *in* the world, holy compassion is our *offense* against indifference and irrelevance *to* the world. It's time for God's Holiness women to step up their offense. We must not quit until we have dethroned the reigning champion of sin and evil. We must step up in the name of the Lord, communicating God's will to others, as the wise woman of the city of Abel Beth Maacah did in the Old Testament days. Take the time to read the story of this incredible woman in 2 Sam. 20.

To make a long story short, a man named Sheba rebelled against King David and wreaked havoc throughout Israel. This one man was a menace to the peace and well-being of Israel. David recognized Sheba's destructive power and sent his captain, Joab, along with his most able men, after this renegade.

Sheba found a hiding place in the city of Abel Beth Maacah, a well-fortified city. The slick rascal disguised himself well enough to blend in with the townspeople. Because the city was so well protected, Joab and his army tried to break through the wall with a battering ram. While they were battering the wall, one individual stepped up and put an end to the nonsense. This sagacious woman told Joab there was a better way to get the enemy Sheba. He wouldn't have to knock the wall down. Sheba's head would be delivered over the wall of the city by this wise woman's hand. How would she do it? By communicating a plan of wisdom and justice that would bring peace to all concerned. They listened to her wise advice and together cut off the head of Sheba the menace—and as promised, she threw his head over the wall.

Am I advocating that you cut off the heads of those who wreak havoc in our homes and communities? As tempting as that sounds, God's way is "not by might nor by power, but by my Spirit, says the LORD Almighty" (Zech. 4:6). Yet we must recognize the danger of our enemy. We cannot afford to fool around with this rebel. The peace and well-being of this world depend upon our willingness to engage in wise strategies that derail the devil's evil plan and defend God's holy plan. I'm calling on women to step up and, with the wisdom of the Holy Spirit, take over their homes (Jerusalem), neighborhoods (Judea), cities (Samaria), or wherever they go (the ends of the earth) (Acts 1:8), in the name of our holy Lord.

28

THE HONOR OF YOUR PRESENCE IS REQUESTED

The tension between the defensive posture of personal holiness and the offensive position of holy compassion is not easily maintained. Countless arguments and debates have ensued over which is more important—relational holiness or functional holiness. Relational holiness is more concerned with how the person relates to God's character, or what one *is*, whereas functional holiness emphasizes the impact a Spirit-filled person has upon his or her world, or what one *does*. God's call to holiness does indeed emphasize the *who*. We're instructed to *be* holy. However, we also see a *doing* in the being.

Many people feel relational holiness is shrouded in an overabundance of rules and regulations—"dos" and "don'ts" (actually more don'ts than dos!). It's almost as if there were an official list of characteristics, habits, relationships, places and things that can be checked off; and if those are successfully engaged or disengaged, whichever the case my be, then the person is deemed to be "holy."

However, if holiness is ultimately about love, the question becomes: "What must one do to quantify his or her love?" There's a "look" of love, if you will. What is the "look" that Holiness women should present to the world?

Jesus seems to suggest that the "look" of holiness can be found in the correct responses to the situations and questions posed in Matt. 25. Jesus declared it to be like the five wise virgins whose spiritual lamps were constantly prepared to give light in darkness (vv. 1-13), or like the servants who multiplied the talents they were given rather than hiding them, thereby rendering them useless (vv. 14-30). Ultimately, the present-day "look" of holiness can still be lived through the challenging dialogue recorded in verses 37-40. We Holiness women must constantly evaluate our spiritual lives against this conversation.

"Lord, when did we see you hungry and feed you, or thirsty and give you something to drink? When did we see you a stranger and invite you in, or needing clothes and clothe you? When did we see you sick or in prison and go to visit you?" The King will reply, "I tell you the truth, whatever you did for one of the least of these [sisters] of mine, you did for me" *(vv. 37-40)*.

Stop and ponder these personal questions: What am I doing with my spiritual oil (or light)? Am I using insights gained through my personal experiences to help someone going through a similar situation? Or do I remain silent, afraid of rejection or the added responsibility? How do I compare? Who am I like— the five wise virgins or the five foolish virgins (vv. 1-13)?

What am I doing with my time? Do I feed the hungry? Do I satiate the thirsty? Do I give hospitality to the stranger? Do I clothe the naked?

We have been blessed so we can *bear fruit.* We were created anew in Christ Jesus with the same charge that God gave to our mother Eve: be fruitful and multiply. Replenish the earth. How will our fruitfulness be made manifest? How do we replenish the earth? We must replenish the earth by pouring our lives into other women. We must communicate the word of love and power to those in the earth so that they, too, may know God's power and blessing. Our holy lives must impact every person we encounter. Other women will know more about their sacredness because we have impacted them, because they have received a touch that brings deliverance.

When people are released into their sacredness because of our witness, we are bearing fruit. The holy cycle is then set in motion. Released people will communicate the power of sacredness to others, who in turn will be set free. The earth is being replenished and restored to its sacred calling in God.

Your story of grace is the greatest asset you have for communicating holiness to others. Your personal story of development, deliverance, and destiny will do more to release people to fulfill their sacred mandate than you'll ever know. Stories are powerful. That's why Jesus spoke so often in parables. People understand a good story. And there's no story as "good" as one that you have personally experienced.

Sister, you have a powerful ministry—the ministry of "telling." You have been called by none other than our Savior to share your firsthand report of how God's power can re-create and restore a broken life. It happened to you. You survived that tumultuous, adulterous relationship. You lived through the defamation of your character. You came out of the tunnel of depression. You tore off the burial garments your life situation delegated to you. You refused to die. You *chose* to live!

What are you doing with your witness? To whose life do you bring the liberating light of truth? You have the light of the Word of God and the light of your experience. So I ask you again—What are you doing with your witness? How are you using your light?

You may be saying, "But, Lady Di, my light is just a small, flickering candle with no more intensity than a match. I don't really have much to tell. Who would want to hear my story?" My response is simply to ask you a question. Have you ever been in a dark room with nothing but a box of matches? Then you know how bright a match is in the middle of an utterly dark place.

We're called to be the light of the world. We're called to be witnesses for Christ in the world. And you, my sister, have been chosen by God to fulfill this specific assignment. It is not enough to "be" holy unto yourself. You must allow your life to be an effective channel through which God's grace flows into others' lives in the world. What the world needs is an authentic witness of holiness—*your* authentic witness.

You must be present and accounted for. Your presence will make the difference. The Lord fervently requests your presence, and the world *urgently* needs it—now.

29
CHANGED OR CHAINED?

———————————●———————————

Women need to hear the stories of other women whose chains have been broken by the power of Jesus Christ. Sisters need the testimony of other sisters whose lives have been changed by the Holy Spirit's infectious power. I've said it earlier in this book, but it bears repeating—there are some messed-up, truly hurting women in this world. Many of them sit in the pews of churches week after week. Many others would never darken church doors for various reasons. Most of those reasons surround the idea of unworthiness or being unacceptable in church circles.

What these hurting women need most is a real-life encounter with the living Lord. They need to hear the message of the hope we have in Jesus Christ, who offers the cure to meaninglessness and despair. Who best to share that message than those who have heard it themselves? I once heard someone say that God wants to take your *mess*—the difficult conditions through which you have come—and give you a *message* that He can use to break the chains of someone's bondage.

Through Christ, God specializes in bringing a mighty conclusion out of a messy condition. Let's go back to the account of the Samaritan woman at the well (John 4:1-42). Jesus was getting into some real "problems" by (1) going through Samaria, a feat that showed unmitigated gall (no God-fearing Jew would set foot in the province of Samaria) and (2) talking to one of its residents. Speaking in public to a woman (any woman, including one's own wife) was a shame and a disgrace to any Jewish male. At first glance, this was turning into a very messy situation.

Realize this, however: Jesus was not about to accept the status quo. He came to *change* anything and anyone who didn't fit into His kingdom mission, to bring the kind of change that broke chains and released people to fulfill their holy agenda.

So Jesus went to Samaria. He also took His disciples. The Samaritan woman was a definite candidate for this mission. By the time she talked with Jesus, this woman had become a moral outcast. She had been married to and divorced from five men and was now living with another. Keep in mind that women of that day could not initiate divorces. Only men could terminate a marriage. Five different men kicked her to the curb by ending their marriages to her. Talk about feeling rejected and unwanted!

Strangely enough, after five divorces, this woman had not quit looking for love. She was definitely chained to the need to have a man in her life.

Obviously, this Samaritan woman felt a thirst that had not been quenched by five husbands and a live-in lover. It was greater than the physical thirst that caused her to take the daily walk to Jacob's well. This inner thirst was so great that it led her to talk to yet another man, a Jewish man at that. This was strictly forbidden in her culture. But, you see, that's the funny thing about unrecognized spiritual thirst. It can be so pungent that it will drive us a long way from home to seek satisfaction.

Jesus offered water that would break the cycle of dependency that had led her to the wrong wells for satisfaction. Her life may have been a *mess*, but Jesus had a *message* for her:

> Everyone who drinks this water will be thirsty again, but whoever drinks the water I give [her] will never thirst. Indeed, the water I give [her] will become in [her] a spring of water welling up to eternal life *(John 4:13)*.

This woman's encounter with the living Christ and the life-giving truth He spoke was enough to free her from the shame of her loose living. She had been looking for love in all the wrong places and found it in the least likely place: inside her own heart. Jesus did not condemn her. He simply corrected her vision of herself.

This moral outcast ran from that well at which she met Jesus and declared her message of deliverance. She had truly been changed—and when that happens, the tongue is unchained. When change truly occurs, we will freely tell what God has done for us. I'm afraid that far too many Christians have not truly experienced change. Many have switched lifestyles but are still not changed. They no longer smoke, drink, curse, or do other "worldly" things. They follow good church order, but they are still not changed. Most Christians make only cosmetic changes to their lives. They simply switch worlds. They go from "worldly" addictions to "church" addictions.

But Christ did not come to make us good church members. He came to make us disciples who would do more than change worlds. We would change *the* world, turning it upside down (or right side up, maybe?) in the name of Jesus. In fact, those who are truly changed will be compelled to give a testimony that makes a difference in this world.

This woman's testimony was so compelling that many other Samaritans in her town believed in Jesus and received His life-changing message for themselves (John 4:39, 42). The townspeople must have seen that a definite transformation had taken place in this woman. This was not the voice of an intoxicated person. To the contrary, hers was the sound of one who was under the influence of the holy presence and power of Jesus! His presence in the lives of people is the only thing that will make the difference between being changed and remaining chained.

It is interesting to examine how Jesus even met this woman. It was certainly not a chance meeting. What most consider as happenstance is simply God working incognito. It was indeed providence, God's plan, that brought them together. But Jesus had a lot to do with the progress of this plan. What if He had decided not to go to Samaria? What if He had chosen the tranquillity of tradition rather the courage of convictions? Where would that Samaritan woman and all the people of Sychar be today? Thank God that Jesus moved by the Spirit of holiness and not by the spirit of fear. He was a holy change agent.

What can we learn about being change agents from this situation? First, *Jesus challenged tradition in order to present truth.* He didn't belong in Samaria, according to the religious rules. Yet He chose to risk criticism rather than to remain chained to a pointless tradition. True holiness also frees us to do this. By challenging tradition with truth, Jesus found a woman chained by her own tradition. It was the truth that set her free indeed.

Second, *Jesus challenged social systems that keep people chained.* According to the social rules, Jesus had absolutely no business talking to this woman. None. She was a Samaritan, a female, and a social outcast. Any one of those conditions precluded Jesus from interacting with her. Since the woman was alone at the well, she obviously had no friends. The women of her day traveled to the wells with female siblings or friends. Yet Jesus not only challenged the social rule of exclusion by befriending her but also found a way to correct her faulty thinking without condemning her.

That's not easy. In the name of holiness, many Christian women have totally disconnected themselves from unbelievers and often from those who are simply socially different, such as by race, economics, education, living conditions, and marital status. Some married women are afraid to interact with or befriend an unmarried woman, fearing the influence the single woman may have on her husband, or even the negative reactions of her husband to her having a friend who's not "tied down."

Extend yourself to women who are socially different from you. They, too, need the warmth of your holiness that shows them you love them as they are but refuses to leave them that way. Unjust social systems that relegate certain women to the margins of society because of their social conditions must be challenged and changed. Unjust laws, whether legally scripted or traditionally encrypted, must be overturned.

God wants to use you to release women from social conditions that keep them from fully connecting with God and with God's people. Go—make disciples, even of these.

Give a woman the opportunity of change by letting your light unchain her. Teach her—that's how you'll reach her. Teach her what you've learned through your life situation, as we talked about in the last chapter.

Open your home for Bible study. Establish a support group for women who have suffered physical or emotional abuse. Begin a ministry of healing, sister to sister. Invite a lonely woman to your home for dinner. Send her a card, a note, an E-mail message—something, anything, to let her know that she doesn't walk alone. Throw your arms of love around that woman who has AIDS. Walk with the woman who is captured by chemical addictions. Help a young struggling mother. Teach her what you know about finances and career planning. Challenge unjust systems that relegate groups of people to the bottom because of their ethnicity or gender or social status. Start a letter-writing campaign to your legislators concerning laws that are oppressive and unfair. Get out of your cathedral. The world needs your light. You have within you the light of chain-breaking change.

Don't hide your light in fear under a bushel. Some woman is succumbing to the pain you survived. She needs your light—the light that breaks chains.

30
THIS IS WAR!

As Holiness women of God, we must be fully aware of what's going on. This is war! We're in a spiritual battle with the same deceitful enemy our mother Eve encountered in the Garden of Eden. Until recently, the words "war" and "women" did not go together in most countries. Women didn't go to war. They stayed home and kept life going while the men went off to fight.

Few of us would choose to be in a war. But if you're a member of God's family, you're in a war whether you like it or not. You did not choose it—it chose you. Eve's enemy, Satan himself, is your enemy, too, and he has declared war on the kingdom of God. Holiness people are his archenemies. Why? Because our job is to stop him from doing his job. What is his job? To steal, kill, and destroy (John 10:9).

Women must enlist in this holy war and fight as never before. Remember—you're not blessed and highly favored just to be blessed and highly favored. You're to be a part of the army that will wage war against Satan's destructive tactics. One of his most effective weapons is distorting and destroying God's holy vision in people. Satan knows where there is no vision, people panic in fear and will ultimately perish in hopelessness (see Prov. 29:18).

Light gives vision. It exposes the enemy for who he is. He's not much at all! The light of holiness within you is actually a declaration of war on Satan. Yet remember this: Satan is no match for God's holy women. I believe women have an extra sense of where Satan is moving, often called intuition or a sixth sense. Women have been beating up on Satan ever since Eve called him out for who he was in the Garden—a deceiver, the father of lies.

My sister, Satan was made your eternal enemy in the Garden of Eden. "I will put enmity between you and the woman"

(Gen. 3:15). Satan is trying to draw you into a place of isolation, ignorance, and indolence so he can knock your light out.

When I was in grade school, every one of my classes seemed to have a bully (no, I was not the bully, though I was often her target!). The bully would try to ambush an unsuspecting girl by drawing her into an argument. Her intent was to catch the victim up in the argument so she would have reason to beat the daylights out of her prey. She would start out by saying a few derogatory words about her victim. If that didn't work, she would reach deep into her arsenal and pull out well-known fighting words: "Your momma!"

Only God knows why those were such infuriating words. No matter how afraid the individual was of the bully, when those strategic words were spoken, the fight would rise inside of them. It's as though the victim decided, "Enough is enough. Talk about me, but don't talk about my mother! That's where the line is drawn."

I believe that Satan, the Church bully, taunts many of Eve's daughters even today. He essentially has said, "Your momma!" He's snidely saying, "You're just like your mother, weak and easy. I'll get you, just like I got her. Your momma!"

Some of you have heard the hissing taunts of the evil one. "You'll never amount to anything. Nobody will ever want you when I leave you!" You remember them. You've heard them before. That's Satan saying, "Your momma!"

But note this. Though we know what Satan said about Eve, we also know what God ultimately thought about our mother Eve—she was blessed and highly favored. Although she made a dastardly mistake by believing Satan rather than God, God loved her enough to redeem her—and all who would come after her who would follow Him. So don't sit back and let that enemy Satan talk about you or your mother Eve like that. Those should be fighting words. He's your enemy. Rise up and fight!

Satan became not only Eve's enemy in the Garden but also the enemy of Eve's offspring. Speaking to the serpent who personified Satan, God said, "I will put enmity between you and the woman, and between your offspring and hers; he will crush your head, and you will strike his heel" (Gen. 3:15). Now you and I both know that a mother will not stand by when her child is assaulted. A true mother will find strength from somewhere, any-where, to fight off any enemy who attacks her child.

Women have killed vicious dogs, lifted two-ton vehicles, and even fought others to the death who dared to attack their babies. You can mess with a woman's man, you can bother her money, you can pass her over for a promotion, you can even assault her—but don't you have the unmitigated gall to assault her child. Mother will sniff you out, root you out, and then boot you out when it comes to her baby.

Satan has declared war on Eve's child that she birthed through Mary. Who is that? The Lord Jesus Christ. Holiness is the Christ child alive in you! Where are the women who will rise up in holy anger and say, "Not here! You can't have my child. You can't have my home. You can't have my friend. You can't have my joy, my peace, or my hope. In fact, Mr. Satan, you can't have anything that God gave to me. I'm blessed and highly favored. You are cursed and very much dead. Get behind me, Satan!"

I ask again—Holiness women, where are you? Your child is under attack. Are you a true mother who will rise and fight the battle for truth? Holiness requires it. In fact, holiness demands it. Don't get in collusion with the world by becoming used to sin and worldliness. Fight with truth and light.

PART 6—Conferring

31
ADDING A BLESSING

God's weapons for waging war are so different from ours. In fact, they are often some of the best-kept secrets around. What are those weapons? People, Holy Spirit-filled people. These remarkable "secret" weapons are strategically positioned in the most unexpected places. Their impact is amazing, and the results are eternal.

For example, who would have thought that an elderly widow would be used as such a powerful force in heaven's arsenal? Naomi's return from her desolate journey in Moab could have left her permanently desperate and broken. Instead, she was resurrected from the grave of despair to become a great-great-grandmother of the greatest king ever to rule in Israel (Ruth 4:18-22). Through this dynasty the King of Kings, Jesus Christ, was born.

Yes, God's weapons are different indeed. Think about it. A single, lowly woman from Nazareth gave birth to heaven's most powerful weapon in this war against sin and darkness. This is so amazing. No one would have suspected a single, lowly female to be a viable plan for this war! Yet Mary's selection broke open the floodgates through which empowerment for living would be perpetuated from generation to generation (Luke 1:48). A woman whose name would never have been known in history gained a name and a place that would never be forgotten.

Two women: one old and widowed, the other young and single. Secret weapons indeed! How did these two get linked together? What did they have in common? I believe it was *the bless-*

ing! Ruth blessed Naomi, and she moved from *bitter* to *better.* Elizabeth blessed Mary and started a melody of empowerment that reverberates even today. How has God changed the world for good? It has happened through people who, by the power of the Spirit, have lifted their mouths and hands as instruments of blessing in others' lives.

Take your own survey of the Bible and read some of the blessings biblical people have pronounced upon others. You may want to begin with Elizabeth's blessing to Mary. She spoke volumes into her cousin's life as she loudly proclaimed:

> Blessed are you among women, and blessed is the child you will bear! But why am I so favored, that the mother of my Lord should come to me? As soon as the sound of your greeting reached my ears, the baby in my womb leaped for joy. Blessed is she who has believed that what the Lord has said to her will be accomplished! *(Luke 1:42-45)*.

The blessing conferred by a human voice caused Mary to fully embrace her God-given blessing. What a treasure Elizabeth gave to Mary—a blessing! Instead of mockery and derision, instead of a hundred ways in which life was going to deteriorate at warp speed, instead of anything negative, Elizabeth spoke words of value and honor. She recognized God's hand upon this single, pregnant woman and blessed the work in progress. Elizabeth readily understood that God had a future and a hope for Mary. And so, she gave Mary what she needed—honor, dignity, value. Elizabeth knew it. Mary was a blessed and highly favored woman indeed.

Can you imagine the empowering energy that flowed between those two women? Right then the forces of darkness were dispelled, and the light of hope was revealed. Women, blessing other women—it's an old weapon, but still powerful.

Imparting a word of blessing gives empowerment. When women truly believe they have a hope and a future, they gain the power to conduct themselves as the holy and blessed "cut above" people they are. Does this happen overnight? Not for most! Yet one person's words of blessing can open the channel of faith and belief in someone else. Elizabeth changed the world with one blessing. She had no idea of the full impact. She just blessed!

Who will speak the word of blessing into their lives? Who

will remind them of their sacred calling? Who will be their Ruth? Who will help them see that their name is not Mara but Naomi, not bitter but sweet? Who is their Elizabeth? Who is affirming God's blessing in their lives and conferring an added blessing upon them? Who is speaking to them what God has already graciously spoken, that they are blessed and highly favored, not because *they* are so good, but because God is?

I have talked with many women, Christian and non-Christian. If you simply take an exterior view of these women, you would never suspect how wounded they really are. Their outside personae do not show the inner pain that daily accompany them. Some are high-ranking public officials; others are truly gifted and anointed to serve in their gifting. Some are married and others single. They are making a difference for others. Still, a common thread of pain, brought on by the misperception of their true selves, connected all of them.

One woman struggled with a call to pastoral ministry. The crux of her struggle was common. Can a woman be called to ministry? Many women have been down that road of doubt. But her situation had a slightly different twist. She was single—divorced. Several of those she had gone to for counseling suggested that those "problems" (being a female and divorced) were too difficult to reconcile for ministry.

Yet she knew she had been called! The guilt of not answering the call had become almost unbearable. How would she reconcile this pain? Her answer came, she told me, through a sermon of mine in which I spoke a blessing to the listeners. That sermon dealt with the call of Mary and the blessing of Elizabeth. Mary was single, but she was called. Her call came directly to her, not through Joseph or anyone else. Therefore, the answer to that call could come only from Mary.

This woman I know accepted her calling and decided to plant a church—since the church in which she worshiped refused to affirm her. A word of blessing empowered this woman to rise and address her God-given purpose.

Other women have struggled with the idea of purpose and place. The pain of seeking to balance those tensions with others' unending expectations is often overwhelming. Add to this that many women live in a context that is less than affirming, and the atmosphere for self-deprecation is ripe. Yet from time eternal, God has used the power of a blessing to clarify vision, restore hope, and encourage hearts.

Before God ever breathed the divine breath of life into humanity (Gen. 2:7), God breathed a blessing on them (1:28). From the very beginning, God let it be known that male *and* female were highly valued and greatly trusted. God obviously had great expectations in mind for those dust-molded creations. The tremendous power of that blessing was inherent in God's hope for all humanity.

In His final act, Jesus breathed on the disciples and said, "Receive the Holy Spirit" (John 20:22). In a sense, Jesus was repeating the act of blessing conferred upon the male and female in the beginning. The presence of the Spirit would restore the disciples to their created place of blessing and empower them to live as God intended. God conferred blessings. Jesus, the express image of God, did as well. Conferring blessings seems to have a high priority with God. What, then, could be more Godlike than for those who bear God's image to do the same? One of the holiest tasks we can perform is to add a blessing to someone else.

Imagine what would happen if those who recognize themselves to be blessed and highly favored would begin to confer that same blessing upon others. What would happen if that divorced woman who camps on the back pew of the church out of sheer embarrassment met a Ruth? What would happen if that single young girl who has had so many partners that she honestly can't explain the paternal beginnings of her child met an Elizabeth? What if she truly knew that God still had a plan for her, a future and a hope?

Imagine the power your blessing can release into the lives of women, helping them truly come to know who they are. I'm not suggesting that we grasp for straws and turn fiction into fact. I am suggesting, however, that facts are not always the truth. The fact may be that a person possesses weaknesses and negative aspects, but the truth is that this one is more than what she has become.

Women will have plenty of opportunities to hear about the negative aspects of their lives. The world will see to that! They don't need condemnation—they need affirmation. Even Jesus was sent by God into the world not to condemn the world, but to save the world (John 3:17).

Women need to hear so badly that no matter how bad things may be, they are still blessed and highly favored by God. They have a future and a hope. Don't get hung up on their "before" picture. Through the eyes of love, see the after shot. What they are today is far from what they can be tomorrow. Confer a blessing that helps them fashion their vision so they, too, can see their glorious future.

I ask you, into whose life are you breathing a blessing? How actively do you help other women connect with the God of blessing? I urge you to believe God's report about you. You are blessed and highly favored. Tell yourself, and in the power of the Holy Spirit, tell your sisters today.